T0023220

"This book is a must-read at a time when we absolutely need more successful strategies for navigating conflict and difference. Using specific practices, personal experience, and the core teaching of compassion, the authors lead the reader to a place of transformative engagement. It is an invaluable contribution to evolving our approach to difficult conversations."—Jules Shuzen Harris, author of *Zen beyond Mindfulness*

"In *Compassionate Conversations*, Diane Hamilton, Gabriel Wilson, and Kimberly Loh have offered us a potent gift that can transform our approach to difficult conversations about the things that matter. Humble, clear, and heartwarming, the authors draw on modern neuroscience, developmental psychology, and personal stories from decades of professional experience to weave together an innovative, nuanced, and practical exploration of our humanity. This book is a must-read for anyone interested in bringing spirituality to the realm of meaningful conversation and social transformation."—Oren Jay Sofer, author of *Say What You Mean*

"*Compassionate Conversations* is extraordinary in that it not only addresses the fundamental issues involved in current public debates, it does so using a framework that can actually unite and integrate the various parties in the fractured culture wars. This book shares a series of incredibly useful skills to help you advance genuinely compassionate conversations and find a way to make room for all the parties that are engaged in conflict."—Ken Wilber, author of *A Brief History of Everything*

"The world today needs this book. It's a deeply worthy exploration of differences and identity with perspectives and skills that you and I can learn and practice for life-affirming communication and inclusion. The authors skillfully engage their unique cultural, ethnic, and spiritual perspectives to confront the perplexing questions of how we, as individuals and as a society, can have wise and compassionate conversations. Truly an exciting book for our times."—Wendy Egyoku Nakao, Zen Center of Los Angeles

"There is a depth of wisdom and practice in this book that makes it unique and necessary. It grounds the conversation in Zen wisdom of who we fundamentally are and how we can claim that awareness as we engage in the challenges of being together in deep conversations. It brings this wisdom to our current divisive challenges of intolerance and conflict, including political correctness, social privilege, inclusion, and identity politics. For its clarity and bravery, its deep and practical guidance, its gentleness and fierceness, I wholeheartedly recommend this book."—Margaret Wheatley, author of *Leadership and the New Science* and *Who Do We Choose to Be?*

COMPASSIONATE

CONVERSATIONS

*How to Speak and Listen
from the Heart*

Diane Musho Hamilton

Gabriel Menegale Wilson

Kimberly Myosai Loh

Shambhala Boulder 2020

Shambhala Publications, Inc.
4720 Walnut Street
Boulder, Colorado 80301
www.shambhala.com

Interior design: Greta D. Sibley

9 8 7 6 5 4 3 2

Printed in the United States of America

♾ This edition is printed on acid-free paper that meets the American National
Standards Institute Z39.48 Standard.
♻ This book is printed on 30% postconsumer recycled paper.
For more information please visit www.shambhala.com.
Shambhala Publications is distributed worldwide by Penguin Random House,
Inc., and its subsidiaries.

Library of Congress Cataloging-in-Publication Data
Names: Hamilton, Diane Musho, author. | Wilson, Gabriel Menegale, author. |
Loh, Kimberly Myosai, author.
Title: Compassionate conversations: how to speak and listen from the heart/
Diane Musho Hamilton, Gabriel Menegale Wilson, Kimberly Myosai Loh.
Description: First edition. | Boulder: Shambhala, 2020. | Includes
bibliographical references and index.
Identifiers: LCCN 2019040810 | ISBN 9781611807783 (trade paperback)
Subjects: LCSH: Interpersonal communication. | Conversation. | Interpersonal
conflict. | Justice.
Classification: LCC BF637.C45 H32819 2020 | DDC 153.6-dc23
LC record available at https://lccn.loc.gov/2019040810

To Ken Wilber,

whose expansive vision and pioneering work

invites us into a more inclusive human story.

Contents

Introduction

Conversation has an immense power to deepen our relationships and cast light on our shared reality. Dialogue is the cornerstone of all significant change in society and the basis of our efforts to create fairer, more equitable conditions for everyone. Depending on what we're trying to talk about, however, some conversations can be extremely difficult. We often avoid these kinds of conversations because we often have unsatisfying and, sometimes, damaging experiences.

Whether we are talking about race, gender, politics, or religion, we can easily become entangled in our differences, in our beliefs about right and wrong, and in our views of the issues. With practice, however, we are also capable of doing something else: being fully in the present moment, accessing our goodwill and flexibility, and using conversation as an opportunity to learn and grow together. Our usual approaches to conversation are not wrong, but how often do we come away satisfied with the quality of our speaking and listening? How frequently have we learned something? And how many times have we felt encouraged to keep talking and go further? This book is intended to show that compassionate conversations can happen, even when challenging, and our differences can inform and inspire us, rather than overwhelm and divide us.

As three authors with very different cultural and ethnic backgrounds, we have come together to write this book precisely because of our commonalities and because of our differences. The three of us all work helping people, but in different fields. Diane is trained as a mediator, Gabe's degree is in education, and Kim has worked in the international conflict-resolution field. We believe in the value of sharing our perspectives, especially when we differ. We have seen how much we learn listening to one another and how our views of culture and history have expanded and changed. We have deepened our sense of empathy while working together and have supported one another in taking personal responsibility for our truths. Working together has deepened our commitment to rectifying injustice. We hope reading this book will inspire you in the same way writing it together has inspired us.

This book explores how to develop better communication skills, particularly at a time when conversations can be highly polarized. Our conversations about diversity or inclusion, about equity and fairness, and about power relationships take place in a historical context of injustice, injury, and pain that is difficult to navigate. These conversations are made more challenging by the fact that injustice is still very real. Despite the potential pitfalls and risks, we hope to encourage our readers to embrace the idea that engaging in challenging conversations can result in shared understanding, wisdom, and compassion.

Conversation is, and will remain, one of the most tried-and-true methods of bringing people together. We place our conversation skills in an evolutionary framework, understanding that talking about our differences is something human beings are learning to do in a new way. Neuroscience is helping us understand the role of the nervous system in creating anxiety and how we can lower the experience of threat when in dialogue. Research in adult development reveals that values vary tremendously from person to person and from group to group, and our ability to hold more than one perspective while in conversation also varies. We will see how emotional maturity affects the quality of our interactions and how practicing good communication skills can make a positive difference in conversational outcomes. We discuss basic communication skills, such as listening, reframing, and working with strong emotions, as well as more nuanced skills, such as perspective-taking and working with power.

We include the insights of Integral Theory and Zen study and practice. And although we believe that spiritual insight and practice are supportive of this communications work, one need not follow a specific spiritual discipline to benefit from reading this book.

We want to encourage our readers to explore, take risks, make mistakes, and become more intimate with expressing their own truth, as well as listening to those of others. Most importantly, we want to give you the confidence that these conversations will support your work for change on the issues that mean the most to you. Our hope is that you will try the practices at the end of each chapter and work to improve your conversation skills.

We wrote this book together. We divided the chapters between the three of us, and one of us took the lead on each chapter. Then we each contributed to the draft chapters, offering additional insights, stories, and edits. We chose to write in a single collective voice to reflect the genuinely collaborative nature of our work together and to convey a sense of that to the reader.

All the stories are true. Most are written literally as they happened. Several have been adapted, and the names have been changed. Diane and her assistant, Julia Sati, made the last copyedits before it went to Shambhala for final review.

Writing a book about communication skills that involves sensitive and often uncomfortable topics is fraught with challenges. It is unlikely that this book will satisfy all readers in all ways, and yet we hope that the benefits to readers and to our world will outweigh any shortfalls. For some readers, our treatment of the relationship between conversation and social justice values may not be strong enough. This may be true. We see this as a book about building the skills necessary to have compassionate conversation—a key component in working for social change—as opposed to a comprehensive guide for *how* to make social change happen. There will also be readers who feel the book overemphasizes some values, like inclusion, at the expense of others, like efficacy. Some may complain that it doesn't take into account the vast cultural differences around how conversations function in different settings and what constitutes success. We expect challenges to our views, and we welcome them, and we also feel our practical experience in facilitating conversation has taught us some things worth sharing. We have facilitated all kinds of conversations professionally. This book will cover some of those skills and show readers how to use them in their personal lives.

People have very strong, differing ideas about what success means when a conversation is challenging. It can vary depending on the purpose of the conversation, the context, or the outcome people are hoping for. For us, success means developing clear intention, being open and available to other perspectives, feeling deeply without getting drowned in emotion, exchanging stories and experiences with an open mind, and facing painful truths with a simple commitment to being present and empathetic. Most importantly, we think that compassionate conversation allows our perspective to shift and enables our sense of self to grow through the course of the discussion. We hope that these dialogues have a positive impact on our relationships, families, work settings, and social action.

We have taken the position that we can't grow alone. Despite our differences in culture or nationality, race or ethnic background, sexual orientation or gender identity, religious persuasion, age, and ability, human beings evolve together. To that end, we explore our sameness as well as our differences in order to pose questions and challenge one another, to share our stories, to make mistakes, and to keep going together. This book is for those who, like us, believe in having conversations about our differences to promote our mutual understanding, shared healing, and shared liberation. This book is also for those who are willing to work on themselves in service of inspiring new ways of being together.

Finally, we hope to point to how our conversations can move beyond identity altogether. Since we are all deeply informed by the Zen tradition, we want to help our readers discover a place within themselves that is open and free from moment to moment, where recognition of our open, unconditioned nature gives rise to tremendous compassion for ourselves and others. And while this may be considered by some to be a spiritual privilege, we believe it is a true necessity in a reality where life and death come hand in hand and where the liberation of suffering is the basis of all social change.

COMPASSIONATE

CONVERSATIONS

1 | *Conversations Evolve*

It is you who were here when the Big Bang occurred.
—Ken Wilber, *The Religion of Tomorrow*

Have you ever had a conversation that you wish had gone better? Have you attempted to discuss a topic important to you and afterward wished you had avoided it instead? Have you hoped you could really talk something over and then wondered what went wrong when you tried and failed? Fortunately, we can learn the skills it takes to have a good conversation, even a difficult one, and communicate with authenticity, presence, and compassion. Learning is itself an expression of evolution, and before we explore how we can have compassionate conversations, let's reflect for a moment on our evolutionary history. Seeing the big picture will help us place conversation in an evolutionary context.

Think about this: Fourteen billion years ago, according to physicists, nothing existed. Then an unfathomable event happened—the big bang. When it occurred, the basic elements of our material reality blew into existence. Suddenly, out of complete nothingness, something was born. The universe has been coming more and more fully into being ever since.[1] The earliest glimpses of matter, eventually, over eons, came together to form electrons, protons, and neutrons. Eventually, these clustered together to create atoms; then atoms came together to form molecules.

Ken Wilber is an American philosopher who is arguably one of our era's most influential thinkers. He is particularly known for articulating Integral Theory, a metatheory that helps us think about how to relate to all the domains of human experience, knowledge, and practice. Integral Theory helps us make sense of the inextricable connection between our outside (material) world and our inside (psychological) world. Wilber advises us to remember that each time a new form emerges, it is a staggeringly creative event in the cosmos. As matter evolves from strings to quarks to atoms, and so forth, the pattern reveals a universe mysteriously encoded to move toward more diversity and greater complexity.

In terms of evolution, when atoms eventually organize into molecules, something different and more complex comes into existence. Molecules morph into several different kinds, and those come together to coalesce into cells. A cell membrane forms around these molecules, and suddenly life is born from insentient matter. This occurrence of life is another astonishing event—it is indeed wondrous to contemplate how something entirely new, different, and more complex emerges from something that is already established, simpler, and fundamentally the same! How it happens, we don't know, but *that* it happens is clear. This miracle is the process of evolution that Alfred North Whitehead refers to as the "creative advance into novelty."[2]

From the earliest cells, then, different types of organisms start to build up. Along comes plankton, and from plankton, larger vegetation, both in the ocean and on land. One-celled protozoa evolve into more complex animal life-forms. Fish appear, then amphibians emerge, then reptiles, and then the complex dinosaurs. Invertebrates such as the elegant octopus go through their own developmental process. When the dominant dinosaurs disappear,[3] there is room for mammals to take over, and life-forms, with even more variation and more complex nervous systems, blossom. Through several mass extinctions, life always reemerges, more diverse, more complex, and more resilient.

Vertebrate nervous systems evolve from registering simple sensations and perceptions to a more complex reptilian brain that regulates the body's vital functions such as heart rate, craving for nourishment, and the impulse for protection; to a mammalian limbic system that houses emotions and memories; to a neocortex that provides for reasoning, conscious thought, reflection, and language, including math and music.[4] This unfolding is truly unfathomable. But there's more.

Evolution on the outside corresponds to a simultaneous evolution occurring on the inside, meaning that as life develops a more complex nervous system and brain, it also becomes more self-aware.[5] For example, plants don't seem to have an obvious sense of self, but a dog definitely cowers when we scold him for nosing around in the trash. He appears to have a sense of self seemingly capable of shame, but he isn't plagued by what he has done wrong earlier in the day or worried about his conduct in the future. This kind of complexity needs an even larger brain with a greater capacity for self-concept and a sense of time. As life becomes more self-aware, so do individuals and cultures.

Evolving Humans, Evolving Cultures

Human beings begin emerging in their earliest form about a million years ago, and in modern form about two hundred thousand years ago.[6] As the neurophysiology, brain chemistry, and structure of the human central nervous system becomes more complex, the cultural dimension of human beings also evolves.[7] About 1.75 million years ago, our human ancestors begin making tools, and around the same time these prehistoric people begin to talk, having their first conversations.[8]

Early humans exist in small tribes, hunting, gathering, roaming, warring with one another, and then settling down to create the first cities and farms. Later, they form bigger, more stable nation-states, churches, and ethical codes. Some begin sailing around the world in a flurry of travel and trade. Throughout our evolutionary history, humans live peacefully together, but we also battle, dominate, and subjugate one another.

During this period, the expansion of nation-states results in the oppression of many indigenous cultures around the world, as invaders colonize, planting the flags of their monarchies on foreign soil. The negative impacts of colonization on local cultures are still felt today.

Around this same time the scientific revolution begins to emerge, with its emphasis on objectivity, instrumentation, and measures. It changes some of our most basic ways of orienting, including a repositioning of the earth in relation to the sun. We now contemplate the heavens from a different perspective: rather than looking up at the skies through the filter of religion, we see through the clear lens of the telescope. Galileo gazes up at a vast night sky without interpretations about God or interventions from priests, but with a new tool and a mind wide open to the starry wonders above him.

New scientific, technological, and philosophical insights give rise to industrialization. This period of time generates the sensibilities of modernism, which are reflected in the clean lines of art and architecture of the twentieth and twenty-first centuries. Our newly acquired value of rational thought and reasonable conclusions can be seen in our educational and justice systems. We begin to contemplate more objectively the fair treatment of all human beings in rational terms and create the secular rule of law. Values such as freedom, self-determination, and equality for all become common in our thinking, speech, and constitutions. Slavery and other forms of subjugation begin to be outlawed around the planet[9] (even though, sadly, they still occur today). The scientific revolution, with its technological advances, is also responsible for the rapid change in the general standard of living of human beings around the globe over the last several hundred years.[10]

Modernity transforms the world in many wonderful ways, but it also reveals its limitations. The scientific method is extremely powerful; it results in tremendous medical advances and engineering feats, but does not necessarily answer our existential questions, nor does it soothe our souls. It attempts to see reality objectively, and it succeeds in part, but tends to become blind to its own limitations. The free market efficiently directs human ingenuity, but it also unleashes greed and exploitation on a grand scale. In its extremes, modernity divides the world into winners and losers and leaves a legacy of unexamined trauma. The one who dies with the most toys wins in this unfair, unhappy, and unsustainable game.

So out of modernism arises a different sensibility. Postmodern consciousness in the West first appears in the works of Jean-François Lyotard, Jacques Derrida, and Michel Foucault, which challenge the premises of modernity and how knowledge is produced. Material prosperity creates the basis for aspirations for deeper happiness; now some people have the spare time and money to begin to examine their interiors, observe their thoughts and emotions, and explore their personal relationships. The field of psychology expands beyond psychoanalysis to include humanistic, transpersonal, and even spiritual concerns.

A new kind of self-awareness begins to emerge, as well as an awareness of social conditions. Delving into the psyche to explore the interior of the mind is matched by renewed efforts to address the systemic biases created by colonialism and forms of discrimination, such as race and gender, which persist despite our attempts to create equality. The environmental movement emerges to reveal the grave cost of industrialization: pollution of the air, water, and soil undermines the health of the web of life on which human well-being depends. The burning of fossil fuels and the disruption of the natural balance of the environment culminates in climate change.[11]

Compassionate Conversations

Today, this unfolding is still occurring. Conversations about social justice, diversity, equity, inclusion, and power relationships naturally grow out of this modern rational period in which many people have concluded that all human beings should be treated equally. But rationalism does not go far enough. The modern aspiration for equality does not address the subjective phenomenon of hidden biases or blind spots, nor does it account for the unfair assumptions built into our existing systems and institutions.

Furthermore, it does not examine the dynamics of social privilege and the lived experience of so many marginalized people. These considerations only emerge as a result of the insights of postmodernism.

Many of our conversations today are more complex, imbued with the values of pluralism.[12] We want to talk about identity, including race, gender, ethnicity, sexuality, and ability, as well as the impact of identity on social status. We want power relationships to be made explicit, and we challenge dominator hierarchies so we can overcome victim-oppressor dynamics. We want to expose power abuses and will no longer tolerate collusion with people who perpetuate them. We are genuinely concerned about all forms of social oppression, and we recognize that equality legislation does not transfer equity, nor does it guarantee fair access to resources, security, or opportunities. In our postmodern society we want to acknowledge the actual diversity in our culture and ensure that everyone has a voice and influence. We want to talk about the objective world but include our subjective, lived experience, our feelings and emotions, and we want to cultivate empathy and compassion for others in our conversations. It's a tall order.

Conversations today require more skills, so we must learn and practice them. We need to acquire the flexibility to entertain more perspectives, to listen attentively to one another, and to see truth in our different lived experiences. We must learn to be present to pain and actually *feel* the negative impacts of injustice in the here and now, without becoming bogged down in self-righteousness and blame. This will help us change our culture for the better. We are waking up to a more diverse, more complex, and still sometimes unfair world. This is what we mean by the expression *woke*.

It helps to remember that it is new in many people's experience to attempt to talk about these things, and it's not easy. Think for a moment about how hard it is to talk about the ways you and your family have hurt one another in the past, or how you are still creating suffering for yourself. Think about how you or your partner have tried to address how you do or do not share power and responsibility, or who is in charge of what, and why. It can be stressful. Reflect on the times you've tried to constructively talk about political or religious views at the dinner table, and how it hasn't gone so well.

However challenging these conversations can be, they are emerging naturally in the course of our individual and cultural evolution. Some people instigate the tough talks, others resist; nevertheless, history is moving forward because of these encounters and the corresponding outcomes. They are an attempt to honestly address the truth of how we, as human beings, have wielded power and abused it, in the form of colonialism, patriarchy, the genocide of Native peoples, and the slave trade. To be present to this historical pain is hard. Suffering under its legacy of oppression is even harder. And to address the unjust patterns that persist in today's society is tremendously challenging. But to talk about all of this is worthwhile and necessary.

Because these are not conversations that we have always had in the past, we have to learn how to have them. In the process of learning, we are participating in our growth and evolution. In other words, in addressing our very deep and real differences, our prejudices and systems of injustice, we are creating more complexity, integration, and self-awareness, both individually and in our culture. This much-needed upgrading of our conversations can help in many contexts. In addition to conversations about justice and equity, we need to talk about the increasingly severe climate and ecological crises that we are witnessing on our planet.[13] We need to address the ever-widening gap between rich and poor, and how to function in a more complex global system, where the scale of problems we're facing is enormous. All of these challenges require an evolution of our human consciousness and a significant boost in our communication skills.[14]

We have described the process of evolution in this opening chapter in order to place the need for new conversational skills in an evolutionary framework. This framework reminds us that we don't live in a world of givens, but rather, we are slowly, painstakingly evolving and learning in a two-steps-forward, one-step-back motion of change. We can regard learning these skills as a form of evolution that will, in real time, allow us to participate in a miraculous, immense unfolding that should amaze, inspire, and surprise us, even as it confounds, challenges, and upsets us.

The emergence of new and different perspectives is a hallmark of cultural evolution. Conversations naturally evolve to include more dimensions, and individuals gradually learn how better to have them. Sometimes it's difficult, sometimes awkward, and sometimes extremely frustrating. The fact that new conversations are happening, however, indicates that societies are changing the world over, and the conversations themselves are evidence of this change.

But people vary in their individual development in how they participate in these evolving conversations. Some people have never sat in a room and talked to people with dramatically different life experiences, and have little interest in doing so. Other people are curious and available but are still new to talking about differences. They often participate like beginners, clumsily sometimes, aggressively now, defensively then, and they stumble easily into some of the pitfalls that being new poses.

Others are very seasoned participants who are able to have fruitful conversation. But there are those who are also advocates, and they often have strong views about what is right and about how people should express themselves. They are quick to call out errors or insist on politically correct language that can interfere with the flow of conversation.

And there are some who are extremely experienced, with agility at taking perspectives and a capacity for nuance that everyone can learn from. They are both energized for change and patient in the extreme. They are fierce and gentle, challenging and merciful, and willing to take a strong stand while adapting to what is needed in the moment. For these participants, conversations are an expression of compassion.

In any one conversation there can be quite a mix of experiences. But what all of us have in common is the capacity to learn, to grow, and to change our thinking. So, no matter how new or experienced we are in having difficult conversations, and no matter how well or how poorly the conversations go, people are trying and people are learning. Learning is itself a form of evolution, and although sometimes it's hard to believe, we have faith that humans are changing for the better.

THE PRACTICE

1. Consider your own evolution. What are the ways that you have grown and changed in your life so far?
2. What are one or two ways in which you would like to evolve?
3. What kind of practice will you have to undertake to bring that evolution about?

2 *What We Have in Common*

In a moonlit night on a spring day, the croak of a frog
pierces through the whole cosmos, turning it into a single
family.

—Chang Chin-Ch'en,
"On a Moonlit Night while Imprisoned in Chang'an"

We believe that a conversation about our differences should begin and
end with an acknowledgment of the myriad ways we are the same. Talking about our differences is urgent, exciting, and even dangerous. But our
commonalities appear to be so numerous as to be beside the point, part
of the status quo, or so obvious that talking about them might be predictable, boring, or even worse, sentimental. It's difficult to see with fresh eyes
and appreciate the depth and span of how much we all share.

Diane's thirty-year-old son, Willie, who has Down syndrome, has a
particular fascination with what we have in common. He never takes it
for granted; in fact, he remarks on the commonalities he sees around him
all the time. Once when he and Diane were watching *The Wizard of Oz*
together, he said somewhat out of the blue, "You and Daddy have that in
common."

"What do we have in common?" she asked him, not following his train of thought.

"You are both scared of the wicked witch. You have that in common."

Once he commented as they were driving past a golf course, "Mark Mariani and Uncle Rick play golf, too, with Dad. They have that in common."

"True enough," she said.

Upon hearing the news that his sister's old dog had died, Willie observed, "Mr. Apple and Ali are two dogs who died already. And now Maggie. That is something in common."

"Sure is," Diane said. "And it's really sad."

When he heard Diane talking in somber tones on the phone to his aunt about his twenty-year-old cousin's recent cancer diagnosis, Willie said, "You are just like Daddy and myself. We are both worrying about Stella because we have that in common."

"You are right about that, Willie."

Willie recites these commonalities frequently. Some are delightful and some are devastating, but Diane appreciates that he points them out because she often fails to notice them herself. She says she forgets that she and her ex-husband have something in common—but it's true: they're both scared of the wicked witch.

It helps when we are struggling with other people to remember how much we have in common: We were are all born into human form, and we will all die someday, not knowing how we arrived here or when the day will come that we will pass on. We can see that we all eat to survive, knowing how good food tastes—especially when we're really hungry. And that we all drink water to stay alive, and on a very hot day we prefer nothing more. We can recall that we all have hopes and dreams. We all seek warmth when it's cold and a comfortable place to lie down at night. We all tend to cluster with our own style of people, those who share our values, habits, and sense of humor. Even drug addicts deep in the throes of addiction share their needles, flophouses, and stories with one another.

Every single one of us has experienced deep pain or loss and illness of some kind, and each of us has had our heart broken in one way or another.

The Dalai Lama says, "As human beings, we are all the same. We all want happiness and do not want suffering."[1] We would add that even as we've been hurt, we have also hurt others. As Willie would say, "We have that in common."

We Need to Belong

Willie's fascination with commonalities has a biological benefit. They say that throughout the course of human evolution, our ability to survive has depended on our belonging to a group of people like us—our tribe, so to speak. Historically, to encounter other human beings, foreign ones, almost always entailed danger or threat. In our rough evolutionary history we were probably more likely to be killed by a strange human being than by any animal predator in our environment.[2] And if we were kept safe, it was through the protection of our tribe; even now, when we are surrounded by people who think, dress, and talk like we do, we can relax.[3]

This is no small thing. A conversation that happens in an atmosphere of relaxation and openness is a very different conversation than one that takes place in a room with nervous systems dripping adrenaline, poised for fight or flight. The topic may be the same, but when we are even slightly threatened, our attention constricts in preparation for defense, just like our limbs and jaws do, and our ability to reason is impaired because access to our prefrontal cortex is blocked. In other words, when our attention is taken up by our defense system, we are literally prevented from thinking clearly.[4]

Some recent research conducted by Google concluded that the most productive teams at that company were the ones in which team members felt the most psychologically safe.[5] This meant that team members could take risks, make mistakes, and expose their individual vulnerabilities and confusion without feeling like they would be punished or reprimanded. This need for safety is deep in the hardwiring of human beings and is essential, the research found, for creating environments that are conducive to creative, high-performing teams.

The ramifications of this research are so profound that some people now advocate for simply working together without talking about their differences; in fact, there is a tremendous emphasis placed in some circles on "safe spaces." Recognizing our essential sameness, including our shared intentions and goals, and creating a safe atmosphere is fundamental to all effective teamwork. But talking about our differences, taking risks, being challenged and even triggered is how we grow, change, and learn to encounter difficulties together. Sameness is relieving; difference is exciting and problematic, and our work belongs in the tension between the two.

Gabe, Kim, and Diane have a lot in common. We met in the context of Zen practice because we each have deep questions related to meaning and purpose in life, which led us to meditation and Zen. We all work helping people communicate better and facilitating conversations about issues that matter, such as race equity, gender equality, power relationships, politics, and religious divides. We all have had the privilege of being college educated, and even though our respective degrees are in education, conflict resolution, and psychology, we still have tons of questions about how to work with people. And the three of us believe that by listening to those who are different from us, we can learn more. This includes trying on different perspectives and seeing the grain of truth in them, even when they are incomplete, partial, or appear to be just flat wrong.

Our Differences Matter Too

Most importantly, we believe that diversity and social justice work must happen in relationships with those who are different from us, otherwise we run the risk of asserting our age-old tribal habits and being bound up in the intractable power struggles that always go along with exclusive commitments to our own group. A congress that can't compromise can't function, and a politician who remains rigidly fixed to one set of ideas will eventually fail. Creativity and connection results from engaging difference—different viewpoints, life experiences, and values.

Of course, we can advocate for the groups we identify with, too, such as people of color organizing with Black Lives Matter or women organizing for #MeToo, both meaningful and powerful movements in our culture now. And as we work to bring attention to a specific group with a specific set of challenges, we believe that the ultimate goal is for all people to treat one another with dignity and respect, creating equal access to resources and opportunities regardless of our individual and cultural identities. For that, everybody has to be in the game.

We do have our differences. Gabe identifies as male; Kim and Diane, female. Gabe and Diane are straight, whereas Kim's orientation is more fluid. Kim definitely has more tattoos than Gabe and Diane put together. Kim and Gabe are both millennials, while Diane is sixty now. We work together because we want to learn from our different generational outlooks. Most importantly, our differences keep us from presuming that we always think the same way, that we have had the same life experiences, or that we have arrived at the same conclusions.

Gabe speaks English as well as Portuguese because he was raised in the United States, where his black father grew up, and then moved to Rio de Janeiro, Brazil, as a kid, where his mother is from. He went to school in Rio from the age of nine to eighteen and can hang on the beach as well as anybody. He can talk about race relations from both of these cultural perspectives, and he can take the perspective of someone from the Northern hemisphere who has a lot of privilege, and someone from the Southern hemisphere who sees the dominance of the United States in Latin American politics, and its ill effects. He appreciates the abundance and prosperity of the North, but he values the sensuality, warmth, and ability of Brazilians to make genuine contact with one another.

Kim grew up as a third-culture kid, living between the United Kingdom, Hong Kong, and Singapore for most of her childhood. She is adept at shifting between these cultures, but unlike Gabe, who feels at home in both cultures of his upbringing, Kim, at times, feels the tension of living between the cultures of Asia and the West, without feeling like she fully belonged in either. She speaks English primarily as well as some Mandarin, having lived in China as an adult in her late twenties, and she is compelled by a desire to connect more deeply with her ethnic heritage. For her, assuming a single national identity can feel limiting and at times compromising to other parts of her identity. Her antidote to homesickness is feeling at home in her own body and learning to be at home in the world wherever she is.

Kim and Gabe both know the struggles of being a person of color: encounters with bias, unfair assumptions, and real prejudice. Gabe recalls having been called racial slurs; he also has been asked what race he is, and then told he's wrong. Kim remembers analyzing with her sister the various kinds of racism they felt in schools they had attended in different parts of the world. She often changed her response to the question "Where are you from?" depending on who was asking.

In contrast, Diane grew up exclusively in the American West, riding horses in the mountains and sleeping out of doors in Utah. She is of Northern European descent in a predominantly white culture in Utah, and she still lives within fifty miles of her childhood home. She has a natural rapport with nature and with the plants and animals she was raised with. She has the privileges of her cultural background, as well as the pain. The ravages of poverty, alcoholism, and coming home from war have left deeply destructive marks on her family that they are still coping with today. That intergenerational pain is what led her to study conflict resolution and Zen.

Our differences are interesting and not in and of themselves problematic. Gabe alerts Diane at times when she is looking through an exclusively white lens, failing to see how a person of color may see things differently. At times she reminds him that for a woman it might not be so easy to speak up and trust that she will be heard. Kim occasionally asks Diane and Gabe to both slow down, sometimes without specifically saying so, so that she can reflect quietly in a way that includes another worldview. This is one of the deepest values we share—revealing our differences, and not just coping with them. We yearn for a depth of relationship that can be challenging, awkward, embarrassing, and sometimes tense, but when we succeed, these truths fortify our relationship with one another, helping us be more forgiving and flexible.

There have been times when we have all given up on this work because it is so treacherous and fraught with difficulties. Talking about identity, power dynamics, and deeply held beliefs—whether it's race, gender, politics, or religion—is difficult because we each care so much about these issues, and there is so much at stake. Sometimes we joke that the title of this book should be "Better Not to Talk about It." But we have each made the choice to stay in the conversation, making many mistakes in the process and making friends with saying or doing the wrong thing. We have also watched one another falter when working in groups, and there have been occasions when we have spent a lot of time laughing and pulling one another upright again after a complete fail.

We rely on one another's different perspectives in order to see beyond our limited viewpoints, so that we can act, in any given moment, in a way that honors all of us. But this means we have to practice. We have to rouse our good faith, listen intently to one another, ask real questions, and stay present to new perspectives. We must learn to surrender our fixed viewpoints and allow our egos to quake and shudder when we don't agree or when our perspective is challenged. Through encountering the discomfort of the unknown, we have learned to expand and change. We have so much in common to work with, but we are so distinct, individually and culturally, that we need to openly acknowledge our respective differences so as not to be imprisoned by them.

True Commonality

One final thing we have in common: we are all engaged in Zen practice and the question of who we really are. We recognize that it isn't a question that we share with everyone, yet we have each had unique experiences that have compelled us deeper into this inquiry. For Diane, it was the death of seven friends (four died in plane crash, one died in an automobile accident, one was killed in a knife fight, and one committed suicide) in her junior year in high school. She suddenly wondered what, if anything, had meaning in life, given that we are all going to die. For Kim, it was seeing, at a young age, situations of deep poverty in places she traveled with her parents. This provoked questions about suffering and being human. For Gabe, it was developing a heart condition during his sophomore year at Stanford, which confronted him with his own mortality, stole his athletic life, and scattered his friends. We each intuitively found our way to meditation because the practice supports asking the deep question about our true identity.

The Buddha himself went in search of that question: Who am I really?[6] He was born into a family of wealth and social status, enjoying all the pleasures and privileges of his time. The story goes that he was dissatisfied and questioning his life, and so one evening he left the walls of the palace where he lived, venturing outside the boundaries of his known world. In leaving home he was said to have encountered a decrepit old person, a sick person, and a corpse. These were dimensions of life that were disturbingly unfamiliar to him, but he knew that he and everyone else was vulnerable to them. He decided to devote himself to discovering if there was anything in life that was not subject to these conditions.

The Buddha's was a significant spiritual search. He engaged in yoga, practicing intensively with body and breath, and began a meditation discipline. But when he wasn't thoroughly transformed, he moved on. During another period he practiced austerities, depriving himself of food, drink, and any form of comfort. Despite his intense self-denial, he still was unable to attain the unconditional state that would vanquish his search. So he gave up his austerities and began to live according to the Middle Way, neither indulging himself nor depriving himself. He saw that he needed strength and balance to continue with meditation.

Finally, he sat down under a tree in India now known as the Bodhi tree,[7] and he committed to staying there until he had found the truth. After a long period of practice during which he encountered many obstacles in the mind, he was said to have awakened. He realized the Four Noble Truths: the truth of suffering, its causes and endless repetitions, the way to liberate it, and the steps for doing so. He was able to see past the boundaries and limits of his egoic identity so that he perceived clearly that he was both the same as and one with everything else. As the morning star, Venus, shone in the Eastern sky, he was entirely free of any division in his mind or heart. He felt completely at home. It is said that he touched the earth, saying, "When I awakened, myself, the great earth, and all sentient beings together attained the Way."[8]

Spiritual awakening is the deep discovery that we are not fundamentally separate from others, nor are we essentially different from them. Our deepest nature is the same. All of us, the stars and the great earth, and all the various beings in our world, from the tiniest molecule to the immense universe, are one thing. This realization creates tremendous peace in the heart and gives rise to true compassion. In this way we are never strangers to one another, and the circle of care and concern extends naturally to everyone. It is this genuine care and concern that motivates us to write this book and inspires us to stay in the game.

THE PRACTICE

1. Take ten minutes and reflect on the things you have in common with an important person or persons in your life. What impact does the reflection have on you? Try it with someone you feel disconnected from. What impact does this have?

2. Remember a recent conversation that took place in an atmosphere of defensiveness and recall whether it was productive or not. What might have changed if you had acknowledged what you had in common?

3 An Exploration of Difference

> There are no differences but differences of degree between
> different degrees of difference and no difference.
>   —William James, "The Will to Believe"

The word *diversity* speaks to the vast differences between us; differences in our talents, sensibilities, preferences, language, and cultural heritage, as well as our status in human culture—high or low—and our respective privileges or suffering due to that status. Inclusion refers to everyone having a place at the table regardless of role or status, wherever we are having important conversations: at school, in the family, at the negotiating table, in business, in political discussions, or talking about films.

When we explore our differences, acknowledging them, getting to know them, we create a deeper functioning wholeness, equality, and social coherence. Just as evolution is a constant process of differentiation and integration, so human development includes these same waves. We explore our diversity in order to create bonds that can include all the ways we are different.

Gabe was speaking to a friend who hosts a podcast dedicated to conversations that help us think and grow together. Because of his work in diversity conversations, he was invited to be a guest on the program. They were chatting on the phone prior to recording the podcast, going over Gabe's ideas and the values of the host. His friend said he wanted to promote the idea of radical inclusion in our relationships in work contexts and in social action. Gabe agreed about inclusiveness but cautioned, "We can never be really inclusive if we can't address our differences, whether they are economic, racial, gendered, religious, and so on. If we don't, we create a shallow togetherness based on trying to be and stay the same." Gabe was pointing out that the harmony we hope to establish through our inclusiveness is subject to collapse when divisions naturally arise. And since most of us no longer live in traditional cultures that prize belonging above all else, we need to develop our skills for valuing the very real differences that exist between us.

Take a conversation Diane was having the other day. A student of hers who is Jewish reported feeling vulnerable physically, frequently noticing little pains or symptoms, worrying whether something was wrong with her or thinking she might have a terrible illness. She went on to remark that it isn't uncommon for a Jewish person to feel this way. After generations of anti-Semitism, and especially after the devastation of the Holocaust in Europe, the experience of physical vulnerability is very acute in her ancestry. She asked Diane what she thought.

Diane said, "I'm the wrong person to ask. In my culture, we deny illness just as we deny any kind of weakness. My father had a sore in his mouth for a year before he had a doctor look at it. By the time he did, the cancer had moved from his gums into the bone marrow of his jaw, and eventually throughout his whole body. He died from it. So from my perspective, it's intelligent to pay attention to your symptoms. Maybe we can help each other. I'll remind you to relax and not overreact, if you remind me to see the doctor."

From Difference to Oppression

Most differences are not problematic in and of themselves. But how we value or devalue them matters a lot. We ascribe "good" and "bad" to our differences; we are "for" or "against" them, or we find something "better" or "worse" in how we are distinct from one another. For example, you like to get up early in the morning and I don't, and that difference can quickly translate in my mind to *you are disciplined and I am lazy*, or the reverse, *you are compulsive and I am chill*. But the truth is, you like to get up early and I like to sleep later.

But imagine that you come from a working-class background and I come from wealth. I went to elite schools and you didn't. By comparison, you came out on the short end of the stick, with fewer advantages and less access to opportunity. And where access to resources is concerned, there is easily better and worse. But something even more unfortunate goes on as well: the difference quickly translates from externals to internals, from access to opportunity to a measure of one's innate worth.[1] In other words, it isn't that you only have less access to advantages; you are also labeled as being fundamentally less valuable in the eyes of society, and then you are treated that way. This has been shown to have lasting consequences for social status and well-being.[2] So your self-esteem suffers; you may feel shame about where you grew up or about the people in your family. This is a great drag on the spirit that leaves a heaviness in the heart that can be difficult to overcome.

Race is one distinction over which these one-up one-down dynamics have ruthlessly played out. Even though some argue that race doesn't actually exist from a biological perspective,[3] from a social and political perspective the impact of this distinction on people's everyday lives is more than real. From the smallest daily slights to the overwhelming legacies of bondage, imprisonment, and genocide, people of color have been subjected to unfair treatment for centuries in many parts of the world. And while some things have changed, the legacy of past oppression persists in our psyches, social structures, and institutions even now. Thus people of color continue to be devalued, denied opportunity, and discriminated against by our systems. Of course, where there is adversity there is also resilience, creativity, emotional depth, and spiritual strength, but recognizing the harm and rectifying its causes is part of cultural evolution.

It isn't news to anyone that discrimination and the inequities that stem from it can be based on a full array of distinctions. Belonging to a group whose skin color is different, usually darker, is one form. Sexual orientation or gender distinctions are another. Speaking another language with a different national origin, like the French-speaking Québécois in Canada, can be cause for oppression. Religious differences create discrimination, as they have for Catholics in the United Kingdom, the Rohingya in Myanmar, or the Muslims in America. One-down status may derive from class distinctions, like for those people born into low status in the caste system in India. Any group that is poor almost certainly experiences one-down status in society. Queer and transgender people have been conventionally viewed as aberrant and so have been marginalized. Perhaps the one-downs are not an ethnic minority but are from a vulnerable population—children, old people, or people with disabilities are more persistently subjected to negative judgments, devaluation, and mistreatment.

Sometimes today we see biases flip when, for instance, a white male in a university class isn't encouraged to speak up or voice an opinion. Or in the case of Diane's son, Willie, who, when she asked how he liked his new classroom, responded, "I just don't like those handicapped people. You know, the ones with the crutches and wheelchairs." Kind of harsh coming from a kid with Down syndrome, but we are all guilty of it in one way or another. Our categories may change, but the dynamics of who's up and who's down are the same. And they are pervasive, stubborn, and ever-present.

Some of our differences deserve up and down evaluations. Freedom is better than enslavement; a peaceful, equitable society is far preferable to a violent one. But many of our biases are baseless. Skin color isn't inherently better or worse. One language isn't superior to another. Religions each have their part to play. These evaluations are often assigned by the groups who have dominant status, and they provide the basis for more prejudice. That prejudice leads to greater unfair treatment in society, and the unfair treatment coalesces into deeper forms of injustice. Finally, the injustice solidifies into prolonged institutionalized oppression.

This occurs all over the world because as humans we have persistent patterns of noticing our differences and then judging those who are not like us.[4] When we attempt to have conversations about race, gender, politics, or religion, we are not simply talking about our differences. We are also talking about how we value and devalue them, how we wield power, and how we dominate, subjugate, and inflict suffering on one another. Bias, prejudice, discrimination, injustice, and oppression in all of their external manifestations must be addressed continuously, broadly, and comprehensively. We have to do this in media, education, and politics; through leadership and legal work; through changes in policy; by recognizing the difference between equality and equity; and through sustained, committed social action.

While some people would argue that all real change needs to be concrete, objective, and measurable, we assert that the evolution of our subjective reality is every bit as important. Our unconscious patterns of bias and prejudice are deeply ingrained, and we have to confront them and see them for what they are. Without it, society won't really change. We will only change superficially, with the old discrimination surfacing in another form. But as we do this work, we have to be careful not to become oppressors ourselves, because this can and does happen.

This work is not a small task, but it is a worthy one. It is worth our attention; it is worth our devotion; and it is worth our patience. But it also requires good skills so as not to deepen or exacerbate the divisions between us. And we must always seek reliable sources of common ground, respite, and joy in our shared humanity. We need to talk, share our stories, educate one another, and employ the highly personal practices of awareness, patience, and compassion—which, by the way, Willie definitely needs to do.

As a team, our contribution to this work is interpersonal in nature. We help people talk and listen to one another, practice calming their nervous systems, exchange perspectives, heighten their curiosity about one another, and gain new communication skills. We firmly believe that recognizing our differences—talking about them, acknowledging how we value or devalue them while working to change our unconscious habits—contributes to a world where we all treat one another with dignity and respect. As in biological systems, healthy social systems are tremendously diverse, and diversity contributes to our ability to address the many challenges we face together.

Difference Equals Threat

Talking about our differences makes a lot of people uncomfortable, particularly if it means revealing our own private prejudices or looking at injustices in society. Most of us don't want to do it. It isn't that we simply aren't interested; it's that it creates real difficulties in the body. Like a finely tuned radar system, our nervous system picks up on the tiniest difference and responds in high contrast to how it does when we encounter familiarity and sameness.

Surprising as it may be, just discussing differences often feels threatening. Conversations about differences can easily provoke a fight-or-flight response; instead of a dose of relaxing, feel-good hormones, the rush of adrenalin and other stress hormones pervade the body, increasing the heart rate, flushing the skin, tightening the jaws and shoulder muscles, activating the limbs, and even inducing trembling. These are highly uncomfortable sensations. Sometimes people cry. There is often aggression or defensiveness in our voice. It is difficult to listen when there are stress hormones present in the body; access to the prefrontal cortex is impeded, making it almost impossible to think clearly or hold multiple perspectives. Memory is affected, too, sometimes making it difficult to remember that we actually like the person we're talking to. The evolutionary purpose of this bodily reaction is to provide a boost of energy for movement, for a quick, defensive response, and for protection. Usually when we feel triggered our first impulse is to move away or defend.[5]

The spontaneous triggering of the fight-or-flight response is one reason we often have so little success talking when under its influence. Even though we may appear to be communicating, we're really coping with the uncomfortable experience of stress in the body. We may be saying all the right things, but we remain fundamentally guarded, ready to attack or bolt. And to cope with that stress we resort to domination, trying to convince others we're right. We seek protection in our group, collapsing into a simple us-versus-them mentality. Or we withdraw completely because the stress hormones demand it (it is fight or flight, after all). In all these ways, the body's ancient defense system rules the day.[6]

Finally, what makes difficult conversations even more difficult is that they often involve pain, and we don't like feeling pain. Whether it's the pain of recognizing suffering, or the pain of waking up to injustice, or the pain of feeling angry, guilty, or vulnerable, these are highly uncomfortable experiences in the body. It hurts to acknowledge pain, and it hurts to ignore it. The emotions that accompany the pain are also unwieldy. Some people don't want to talk because the issue is too overwhelming to feel fully. Some don't want to be unfairly blamed or made to feel foolish. Others don't want to talk because it's dangerous to expose oneself and risk being labeled angry, troublesome, or bigoted. Others take the risk and feel their perceptions are minimized or denied altogether. And still others are simply straight-up aggressive in their expression, which always heightens the flight-or-fight response in others. So these attempts at talking can quickly become a hornet's nest of a conversation, where everyone walks away feeling stung.

Some studies have shown diversity training to be ineffective.[7] People don't like being strong-armed into reducing their prejudice. In fact, it can lead to increased hostility and bias, not less.[8] We talk the diversity talk, but we don't deal with the intensity of the bodily sensations that come with feeling aggression or feeling threatened and all the other difficult emotions that can come up. But there are several practices that we can employ in our conversations when we feel triggered that will help right away.

The first is to become very interested in the firsthand experience of fight or flight in our own body. We can learn to stay present with that heightened state and get really curious about what the actual physical sensations are. Where are they located in the body? What is their texture and tone? Are they hot or clenching or rushing or throbbing? How do they shift and change? What is our tone of voice? Is there a sudden gripping in the chest or heat around the throat or neck? Can we feel the sensations of aggression rise in the body and throat? Or the opposite: Do the contractions of fear show up in the solar plexus or stomach? Do we sense a negative shift in our feelings toward other people? Does a sense of separation set in? Most importantly, is there a fundamental felt sense that something is wrong?

Now we can employ the breath to recalibrate the nervous system to calm and soothe ourself. We can focus on two specific qualities of the breath: rhythm and smoothness. As Alan Watkins explains in his book *Coherence: The Secret Science of Brilliant Leadership*, focusing on these two qualities will stop the production of cortisol and adrenaline in just a few minutes.[9]

To breathe rhythmically means that the in-breath and out-breath occur repeatedly at the same interval. Inhaling, we count 1, 2, 3, 4; exhaling, we count just a little bit longer—1, 2, 3, 4, 5, 6. Repeating this cycle establishes a rhythm. At the same time, we should invite the breath to be even or smooth, so that the volume of the breath stays consistent, like sipping liquid through a narrow straw. If we manage these two qualities for just a few minutes, the breath assists us in staying present to intense and shifting sensations in the body.[10]

Finally, we must remember to use the clarity of our cognition, or thinking mind. We should remind ourselves that while these stressful experiences can be highly uncomfortable (which we often interpret as "bad" or "wrong"), they are natural responses. So we need to evolve in order to witness our defensive patterns, recalibrate our nervous system, and relax into the whole experience. The good news is that through self-observation we can learn how our nervous system works and change our defensive patterning by breathing, relaxing, and learning to stay open. This provides a basis for real conversation about our differences, about our use of power, and about our tried-and-true commonalities.

THE PRACTICE

1. The next time you are triggered, become very interested in your firsthand experience of fight or flight in the body. Stay present. Explore all the sensations in the body without judging or wishing them away.

2. Focus on the breath, breathing rhythmically and evenly. Extend the exhalation, allowing negative thoughts to dissolve. Notice how the bodily sensations become more manageable.

3. Remember to encourage yourself. Remind yourself that by staying present and becoming familiar with your own body, you will create the space for new and different responses whenever you feel threatened.

4 *Intimacy with Identity*

To study the Buddha Way is to study the self. To study the
self is to forget the self.

—Zen Master Dogen, "Genjokoan"

Julia Sati is a friend and a colleague in our Zen study and practice group.
She has a memory from when she was about three years old that is still
very vivid to her. She was visiting her grandmother's house, and her
grandmother offered her a molasses cookie. Julia took the cookie and
spontaneously turned to share it with her aunt. This pleased her grandmother immensely, who remarked to the little girl, "You are so generous!"
The little one immediately burst into tears.

"I'm not generous," she said, "I'm Julia!"

Identity Is Important

Identity is one of the most defining aspects of our personal psychology
and social orientation, and it is studied widely by psychologists, sociol-
ogists, and anthropologists. Identity refers to the "totality of one's self-

construal,"[1] or more simply, the totality of what we recognize as "me." It holds all of our important experiences; it links our past to our future and connects us to our people and ancestors, to their triumphs and struggles. Identity has many different dimensions, including personal, cultural, national, gender, and so forth. It provides stability to our life through its set of orienting beliefs and ideas, collection of memories and stories, roles and expectations, as well as positive and negative experiences. All in all, identity is the story that we tell ourselves and others about who and what we are.

Developmental psychologists have mapped the trajectory of identity through very distinctive stages. At one time, human development was thought to be complete with adolescence. But research shows that it continues throughout the entire adult life span.[2] Some models of adult development are very complex, containing many phases. But in a rudimentary model, identity moves through four basic stages: egocentric, ethnocentric, worldcentric, and Kosmocentric. Through this simple model our sense of self grows from smaller to larger, encompassing more and more experience. As the sense of self becomes more expansive, it also becomes less fixed and more flexible. These developmental waves of identity have powerful implications for conversation, and while they cannot capture the totality, uniqueness, or mystery of any particular person, they reveal certain broad patterns that can help us understand why our conversations often take the turns they do.

Egocentrism

Development through the egocentric stage sets the groundwork for a healthy sense of "I" and is crucial for learning self-care and personal integrity. A healthy ego gives us energy, passion, and permission to love what we love, do what we do, and engage life on our own terms. Ego centrism has the power, raw emotion, and life force of a two-year-old shouting "mine!" At the egocentric stage, we strive for personal power, recognition, and resources for our own survival. Sometimes we just want to be left alone with our thoughts, feelings, and perceptions of life and its challenges. Whatever form it takes, the fundamental point is that we are preoccupied with our own life.

The limitations of the egocentric stage are obvious. Self-centeredness, focus on instant gratification of wants and needs, and relating to others and circumstances merely as a means to satisfy our own appetites and desires are hallmarks of egocentrism. On the one hand, we can be incredibly productive when pursuing our own goals and interests, but to the extent that we ignore other people's wants and needs we eventually lose our connections and can end up quite isolated and alone. The egocentric level of identity isn't "bad" per se, but it is narrow, limited, and usually quite claustrophobic. Healthy development means transcending and including earlier stages, so like nested dolls, even as we grow we continue to experience our basic egocentric needs and desires.

When Diane was a mediator, her job was to help people talk about their disputes, address their shared wants and needs, and assist them in making agreements. She was often challenged by the people who came to mediation sessions but who seemed incapable of taking the perspective of anybody else in the room. They weren't bad people; sometimes they were quite charming, intelligent, or persuasive. But they were consistently self-centered, focused almost exclusively on getting their own wants and needs met, often at the expense of others. Her experience was that highly egocentric participants would measure success in terms of their own bottom line, with little or no regard for a win-win.

There are times when we are all egocentric in conversation. We may be threatened, or stressed, or just tired. We may begin to use our own raw energy and passion to prevail on others to assume our point of view, or we may manipulate or try to work around them. We may find that we are more stubborn, emotional, or controlling than usual. We may feel as though our very survival depends on being entirely right or on getting our own way. When we're in an egocentric mind-set, we may be impulsive and lack the patience to hear someone else's perspective. But when we are rested and relaxed, our egocentric impulse is just what is needed to care for ourself and stay connected to our passion and purpose in life.

Ethnocentric Identity

From the egocentric stage, our sense of "I" or "me" expands to include others. There is an African proverb that says, "If you want to go fast, then go alone; but if you want to go far, then go together." [3] Banding together in groups has been integral to human evolution, but it requires everyone putting the interests of the group front and center. When we accomplish this, we are said to be sociocentric or ethnocentric.

At this level of development, what is "me" includes all the people who are important to me, from my children and family, to my friends, co-workers, and teammates—all the people who give me a larger sense of myself. Ethnocentric identity varies and includes our family, clan or tribe, nation, religious group, or even a business or sports team. Loyalty, team-work, self-sacrifice, and obedience are virtues that emerge when we orient to supporting the people who are most important to us. These qualities may remain with us even as we grow beyond this stage.

Ethnocentrism is sometimes referred to as "traditional." Its hallmarks are order and stability, so its values include adherence to clearly defined moral codes and rules of conduct. The moral codes delineate right and wrong, and the rules emphasize conformity, belonging, and getting along with others. Viewing the world through this lens, we orient to a higher authority, whether it's the church, the Constitution, or a set of com-mandments or precepts. Other hallmarks of this stage are self-sacrifice in service of something larger, deriving strength from tradition and pre-dictability from routines and rituals, and relying on conventional wisdom to uphold the social order. Often, people at this stage of development are highly religious, deeply loyal, and willing to go the long haul with their commitments. For example, armies and military organizations are highly ethnocentric; defending the group is their sole purpose.

The downside of the ethnocentric identity, of course, includes rigidity, as though there is only one truth, and it just happens to be ours. There is little room for exploration or for asking questions, so blind conformity and dogmatism rule, and the oppression of "nonbelievers" and the quash-ing of individuality or independence is also common. Within ethnocentric culture there is also the persistent problem of dividing the world into "us" and "them." While this powerful distinction helps us find safety and avoid threat, most conflicts and wars are the result of ethnocentric groups colliding, whether tribes, nations, religious groups, or even cultural value sets. When armed and angry, ethnocentrism is one of most dangerous forces on the planet.

Julia has a strong relationship to her ethnocentric self. She was raised Catholic in a large extended family in a very coherent Wisconsin mill town. People understood the value of hard work and taking care of your neighbors. Even though she went on to work in corporate America, moved from place to place, married a Muslim man, and even lived in Morocco for a time, these Midwestern American values never left her.

So when she moved to a small town in southern Utah, she felt right at home with the local Latter-Day Saints (LDS, i.e., Mormons). She joined the interfaith council as the one and only Buddhist practitioner, and she noticed right away how easily they organized events and supported one another's projects. The meetings had a very predictable structure that always began with a prayer. The leader came to the meeting with a clear agenda and a working assumption that everyone would cooperate with it, which they did. Sometimes there were discussions, but very few objections, and never any open disagreements. There was an overriding value on harmony and agreement. The meetings were highly efficient and almost exclusively focused on activities, goals, and execution. She enjoyed the immense social coherence, the friendly atmosphere, and the ease of getting things done well.

The problem came when the leadership changed one year. It switched from an LDS woman to the local Evangelical Christian pastor. Suddenly, us-and-them differences started to come to the foreground. He was so identified with being a Christian that he just couldn't deal with a Zen Buddhist in the group, and so he would never address Julia directly. He wasn't hostile exactly, but a little overly domineering with his opinions; his sense of self was limited, and so was his truth.

She also noticed that when the interfaith group held an event in public, he wouldn't greet or acknowledge her there, either. The meetings were now being held at his church, and when Julia invited the group to visit the new meditation hall at the Zen center, he refused to come. The lines between "us" and "them" were deepening and now affecting the harmony of the interfaith council. Actually, the only "them" was Julia. But as this went on, she started to lose interest in the group. Needless to say, she skipped the National Day of Prayer event that year while she waited for the leadership to rotate again. The pastor wasn't wrong; he wasn't bad; but he was deeply ethnocentric.

Worldcentric Identity

The next wave of development that unfolds is worldcentrism. At this stage we begin to identify with all of humanity rather than our own group. We recognize the same aspirations and suffering in ourselves and others and begin to act on the basis of universal human values. We see national, racial, religious, and other differences, but these don't result in hard divisions. The whole enterprise of nationalism, and to some degree "otherness," collapses in our mind. We become more curious and less fearful of others. Our identity is more flexible as we practice taking different perspectives and as we learn to care for people who are wholly different from us. This capacity arises as people are literally able to travel the world and surf the internet. This worldview is literally global.

It is worthwhile to look at two subcultures within worldcentrism. The first is *secular materialist culture*, which emerges in reaction to the ethnocentric traditional view. It relies on empiricism and rationality, and forms the basis of scientific inquiry. Unlike traditional culture, it doesn't depend on an authority outside of itself or on the blessings of a deity or priest. It values individual freedom, sovereignty, and the innate dignity of each human being. This perspective forms the basis of our educational system, as well as our constitution, legal system, and courts.

The gifts of this cultural view are the empowerment of the individual's resourcefulness, ingenuity, and self-determination. We expect hard work to result in material abundance, scientific breakthroughs, and technological achievements. We see this identity in people in businesses and corporations, in the sciences, universities, nonprofit organizations, and sometimes in government roles. The downside of this wave of development is alienation from a meaningful inner life, the all-out rejection of religion and spirituality, and unchecked competitiveness and greed, which is now creating vast inequality among people around the globe.

As worldcentric consciousness matures, it becomes less abstract and universalistic, and more aware of cultural contexts and history, personal differences, and ecological principles. *Pluralism*, another cultural wave within worldcentrism, denotes the values of diversity, equity, and inclusion, and it is characteristic of both progressive and identity politics. It is marked by the emergence of the civil rights, women's, LGBT+, and environmental movements in the United States. This cultural identity goes a step further in working for human dignity by examining the truth of power relationships and abuses. Power structures, dominator hierarchies, and people who wield power unfairly are challenged, critiqued, and sometimes dismantled. Sharing power and resources with marginalized communities and giving a platform to the voice of the oppressed is a major focus of this worldview. It strives for more inclusion, recognizing that more perspectives at the table produce better results. It often employs consensus decision-making and uses politically correct language to demonstrate care for one another. It places far more emphasis on people's emotions and feelings than secular culture does, and on people's history of adversity.

This is the upside of this stage of development. The downside is an overvaluing of people's emotions and personal agendas. There can be an attempt to mitigate discomfort and pain that borders on the extreme as people are easily offended and on the lookout for triggers and microaggressions. This vigilance for microaggressions can often prime people to move too quickly to blaming and shaming others for their communications instead of pausing to consider or understand the intent or underlying meaning of the communications. Sometimes conversations are derailed because personal thoughts or feelings are prioritized over action. Even though inclusion is highly valued, there can be a rigid demand to conform to this worldview that, ironically, marginalizes those who express more traditional or secular views, consequently losing out on the meaningful contributions those views have to offer. From this worldview, you are either "woke" or not.[4]

Once we facilitated a conversation between a director of a natural history museum and her codirector. They had been involved in a large expansion of the museum and were ready to turn their attention to new programming. Both were highly professional women, capable and experienced, who had worked together for a long time. From one perspective, they should have been easy to facilitate because they were both articulate, curious, and extremely good listeners. But their collaboration broke down around the difference between a secular-material identity and a highly pluralistic identity. They shared a worldcentric view but were separated by two very different senses of self.

The director had a PhD in natural science, and she was interested in biology, earth science, astronomy, and physics. She wanted to put all of her energy and resources into building out the hard science side of the museum. She planned for the programs to educate young people in the scientific method, teaching them the power of objectivity and observation, working closely with the university on various research projects.

Her codirector was inspired by the stories and history of the peoples of their area, particularly Native people and their interaction with European settlers. She was less oriented toward the natural sciences, but was interested in anthropology, art history, and cultural studies. She viewed the evolution of culture as a constantly interacting, changing process and was excited by the prospect of teaching young students about the myriad forces that shaped the social structures and art of the early peoples of the place.

From one perspective, their differences could have been highly complementary to the work of the museum. But the two women seemed unable to realize that potential. The director repeatedly extolled the rigors of the scientific method while intimating that her colleague's interest in cultural studies was soft, nonscientific, and preoccupied with the power relationships of the peoples of the past. The codirector affirmed the perspectives of the director but made it clear that she felt the director's emphasis on science lacked soul and was out of step with current trends toward storytelling and cultural relevance.

Worldcentric conversations usually have room to exchange multiple perspectives. People can think in terms of "both/and" rather than "either/or." There is far more curiosity, questioning, and exploring than earlier stages. But when identity is at stake, when we *are* our perspective and our preferences rather than having them, we feel threatened by differences and grip tightly to our own truth in response. Identity is not usually negotiable. We may see others as being well-intentioned but also confused, wrong, or even harmful. Because of the deeper attachment to their respective identities, the two women were not able to create a new vision for the museum together.

Kosmocentric Identity

The worldcentric identity is much more expansive than the ego or ethnocentric identity, but it is still bound by hopes and fears, space and time, and deep attachment to the difficult human enterprise. When identity expands from worldcentric to Kosmocentric,[5] we discover the tremendous spaciousness, stillness, and even silence that pervades our experience. We move beyond our preoccupation with hope and fear and are less bound by past and future. The present is full and meaningful. Usually at this stage we are engaged in spiritual practice, have been through a life-changing experience, or have confronted our own death. We can see ourselves as part of the great flux of coming into being and passing away, and we have trust in the profound process of life and death.

People who have this wider view tend to see our interconnectedness and are not invested in deepening divisions, whether between self and other, us and them, or the world and its problems. Our friend Rob McNamara, a developmental coach and Zen practitioner, says that in contrast to prior stages of development that view conflict as something to be

solved, the Kosmocentric self sees the process of conflict as innate to evolution and necessary for transformation. At the same time, there is more
compassion for the challenges, tribulations, and limitations that each
stage of identity brings.

To call this level of identity the "Kosmocentric self" is not quite accurate because at this stage, identity becomes more fluid, more flexible. We
experience the egocentric, ethnocentric, and worldcentric identities as
rising and falling away and notice much less attachment to them. These
identities are free to come and go, fully inhabited in one moment and
relinquished in the next, depending on circumstances. It's like going to
a soccer game and being full-on for your team, and later forgetting all
about the fact that you're a fan.

Here, finally, we discover the part of ourself that is beyond identity altogether.

There is a Zen story in which an emperor asks a Zen master, "Who
are you?"

The master replies, "I don't know."

At other moments in human development, this "I don't know" would
be tremendously disconcerting. But the Zen master is comfortable in the
face of the mystery of his own existence.[6]

When the Kosmocentric self is present in conversation, conversations
are focused and yet spacious. Listening becomes easier. Patience is natural. We are inspired to work hard, having clear intentions, but are not
attached to rigid outcomes. Life presents itself as a continuous set of challenges, but somehow we feel up to them. We learn to be consistently present and willing to respond to conditions, understanding that suffering
will always be a part of our experience. And we will always be committed to helping relieve it. Urgency and patience, sobriety and humor, ac-
complishing our goals while being fully in the here and now come hand
in hand. We start to experience the paradoxes of life and begin to understand biblically based adages such as "Be in the world, but not of the
world" or "For it is in giving that we receive, it is in pardoning that we are
pardoned, and it is in dying that we are born to eternal life."[7]

The Map, Not the Territory

Research shows that humans go through distinct stages of development that encompass more and greater perspectives; however, researchers don't understand how to support people to move from one level to another. In other words, studies have identified general patterns of development, but how each person walks through this territory is unique.

Each of us must walk the territory of our growth, and there are likely as many ways to do it as there are people on this planet. Even so, the fact that our identity evolves invites all of us to become curious about ourselves and inquire into how we are making sense of the world. We can question what appears obvious to us and what we might be missing or failing to see. We can ask ourselves about our biases and ask for feedback about them. We can be curious about who we agree with or disagree with, and why. How does it determine or bias who I agree with and who I disagree with? We can be curious about our values and priorities and wonder how they can grow or change. This opportunity, we believe, invites all of us to be more intimate and curious about ourselves, and the more intimate and curious we are about ourselves, the more intimate and curious we can be about others.

THE PRACTICE

Explore different levels of identity by completing the following sentences.

As the egocentric identity, what I notice is . . .
As the ethnocentric self, what I am proud of is . . . and what I am ashamed of is . . .
As the worldcentric identity, I am interested in . . . and what I am overwhelmed by is . . .
As the Kosmocentric self, what I am aware of is . . .

5 *What Is True*

The Importance of "I," "You," and "It"

Everyone is entitled to his own opinion, but not to his
own facts.

—attributed to Bernard Baruch

Gabriel's grandmother, Margaret Bush Wilson, was a lawyer, civil rights
leader, and the first black woman chair of the board of the National Association for the Advancement of Colored People. The NAACP, as it is
known, is an organization that has been advocating for the civil liberties
of marginalized groups since the early 1900s. Margaret's commitment to
civil rights, particularly for people of color, was captured during her final
days in the hospital as she went in and out of a coma. Once, when she momentarily came back to consciousness, the one utterance that came out of
her mouth was, "I haven't seen one black doctor yet—we need to fix that,"
only to slip right back into her coma.

As embarrassing as it is for him to admit, when Gabe was a teenager
he thought his grandmother was stuck in the 1950s, fighting a civil rights
battle that had already been won and done. At the time, his perspective
was limited, shaped by his youth, his upper middle-class upbringing, and
by his teenage years in Brazil. His viewpoint was therefore shaped by his

unique value set and colored by his immediate environment. It's not that his perspective was untrue, but it *was* limited—it was particular to him, to his life experiences, and was therefore subjective. He says, "I was operating on an unexamined belief that what was true for me should also have been true for everyone else. I took my first-person perspective as capital *T* truth, when in reality it was simply my truth." At this point he was still unaware of the unique character of racial dynamics and tension in the United States. He also had not yet learned to take a systemic view of the way our structures and institutions promote racism, unjustly and disproportionately impacting historically marginalized people. He didn't fully comprehend his grandmother's commitment to social change, even though he had often heard her say, "Some take the heat so others can eat the treat."

When he returned to the United States to attend college, his worldview regarding race began to be challenged. Sometimes it was through small social interactions, like being asked the question, "Are you black?" This was a question he had never encountered in Brazil. When it happened, he noted how people related to race in the United States—how it seems more important here to fit into a certain racial category and then identify with that category. Other shifts occurred in his mind when he learned about how our government structures and institutions can perpetuate a culture of white supremacy through practices such as voter suppression, gerrymandering, and preventing anyone with a felony conviction from voting, many of whom are people of color.

But the pivotal challenge to his worldview occurred when through the Freedom of Information Act, which provides the public the right to request access to records from any federal agency, he gained access to a series of documents about his grandmother after she died. He learned that the FBI had surveilled her civil rights and social justice work under the guise of "national security." Because she labored to ensure the civil liberties of all Americans, his grandmother was treated as a threat, not to the government, but to the dominant racial group in power: white people. Gabriel says, "This was the realization that fundamentally changed my perspective. I could no longer tolerate the dissonance between my earlier worldview and my new environment, insights, and experiences. My experience of what was 'true' changed as I grew, and my perspectives expanded."

Three Perspectives, Three Truths

Truth is defined as the actual state of a matter, or an indisputable fact, proposition, or principle. It seems like the truth would be the easiest thing for us to observe and agree on. So why do we seem to struggle with alternative facts, fake news, science denial, and general confusion over what to believe? The definition of truth is straightforward, but claims to truth can vary widely and function differently in our conversations and in our culture. Integral Theory helps us think about truth in ways that can allow us to navigate conversations when people make different claims to truth.

There are three fundamental perspectives through which we orient ourselves to truth, and these perspectives determine the pronouns we use in our everyday speech: these are the first-, second-, and third-person singular: respectively, *I*, *you*, and *it*.[1] This perspective filters how we see and what we see and has its own answer to the question "What is true?"

From the first-person perspective, the pronoun "I," truth is simply our own unique viewpoint. It forms the basis of our opinions and is the lens through which we see our lived experience, the ideas we form, and the meaning we make from our unique vantage point in the world. Each of our vantage points is a complex, seamless amalgam of our personal philosophy, neurobiology, genetics, family upbringing, and larger cultural and environmental surroundings. The first-person perspective is not about establishing absolute truth or verifying objective truth, for that matter; it's about affirming that we each have an entirely unique view of the world, and we are entitled to it.[2] But there are many times in conversation when, like Gabe's experience shows, we conflate our first-person opinions with objective third-person truths.

The third-person perspective is not subjective or unique; it is objective truth and represented with the pronoun "it." It is the domain of science and empiricism. Astrophysicist Neil deGrasse Tyson speaks to this often, pointing out that objective truth resides outside of our personal opinions and outside of the built-in biases of our culture, religions, and political affiliations. He reminds us that scientific truths are affirmed through objective methods—measurements, instruments, testing, and repetition—and they exist whether we believe in them or not.[3] For example, the law of gravity is indisputable. No one ever argues with it. The speed of light is a constant, and no matter what anyone says, it stays the same. Energy is neither created nor destroyed, and that won't change based on who holds political power. To establish an objective truth, we use the scientific method: we develop hypotheses, test them, then modify them based on the outcomes. We gather more information and data and continue to modify the hypotheses until they become consistent with what we observe as shown by our testing procedures. The resulting data helps scientists devise explanations and scientific theories.

Truths framed in terms of the pronoun "it" must be verified in this way, and our personal or cultural preferences must be subordinated to them. We must observe these truths from a distance, free of our personal preferences and biases, because distance is central to the scientific method in order to maintain neutrality and unbiased inquiry. This is what we mean by objectivity.[4] It is true that Newtonian physics breaks down at the subatomic scale or as you approach the speed of light, so these laws are not absolute or unchanging in that sense. But the vast array of third-person truths are displayed through medical breakthroughs, engineering feats, and miraculous technologies.

Nonetheless, hard-and-fast scientific facts are often debated in culture by "you" and "me" (the pronoun *you* represents the second-person perspective). Truth is determined in society by what you and I can agree on. Or what we agree on. The "We" perspective, as Diane says, exists in the relationship between you and me—between *us*. Our shared beliefs, cultural values, agreements, and commitments, as well as our ethics, empathy, compassion, and mutual respect all fall into the domain of second person according to Integral Theory.[5] Unfortunately, so does our fighting and bickering, our manipulations, coercion, and violence. Most conflict resolution boils down to facilitating the conversation between *us* about what we can agree to be true.

Take climate change as an example. Technically, scientific research provides indisputable evidence about changing temperatures on the planet, but many people vehemently contest the findings and refuse to take the science at face value. They argue that the climate has changed before, or that it is caused by factors other than the burning of fossil fuels, or that the models are unreliable, or that scientists don't agree. And even when a legitimate survey concludes that there is a "97% consensus (among scientists) that humans are causing recent global warming,"[6] unless society chooses to accept the results of the survey, the facts remain irrelevant in the cultural discourse. The domain of *we/us* is incredibly powerful in this regard, which is why politics overwhelms science all the time.

Using Three Perspectives

Each of these perspectives can be inhabited and utilized for a purpose in conversation. So in our work as facilitators, we do our best to pay attention to which perspectives we are using in the conversation, as well as which pronouns. Sometimes we request that people speak using "I" exclusively. Sometimes we employ the pronoun "we," to test how much we actually agree on. Other times, we will engage a conversation full of objective information, data, or research results, strategic planning, or content expertise. These conversations are full of third-person pronouns, especially "it." In other words, we take a perspective on our perspective, and we encourage our groups and participants to do the same. Let's take a look at a conversation we had recently about gender dynamics. In this case, it involved men and women who work in a technology start-up.

Technology companies generally admit that they are behind the curve when it comes to including the perspectives and sensibilities of women in the workplace. But to their credit this particular company had the aspiration to build gender equality during the early stages of its formation. In the service of that goal, they invited us to facilitate a series of conversations with the founders of the company. It was not our job to determine whether gender bias existed; rather, it was to help the principals talk about their own perceptions and learn better how to raise and examine the issues involved in the different perspectives.

As you can imagine, people in the company had very different perspectives about the dynamics between men and women, and whether women were treated equally, with the same access to position, pay, and influence. We began by inviting everyone to bring their personal "I" perspective to the conversation because, as we said before, everyone is entitled to their own unique viewpoint. It may be wildly unpopular, illegal, or even a little insane, but everyone has a piece of the truth.

When we inquired, some members of the founding team saw no difference whatsoever between the treatment of women and the treatment of men in the company, and frankly they had little interest in talking about it. Others saw no apparent differences but were interested in other people's perspectives. And some saw significant differences, to the point of distress, where one woman was already planning to quit because of what she believed was unequal treatment. Luckily, the conversation didn't stop with the airing of individual opinions, otherwise it would have been quite unproductive. Remember, the purpose of including first-person, "I," perspective is to create a place at the table for each person to participate in the conversation with their own point of view.

While each person has a piece of the truth, these personal perspectives are partially true. And it's important that we distinguish our personal opinions from our shared perceptions and the relevant, verifiable third-person truths in any conversation. So, after hearing from everyone, we moved from the first-person perspective to using the pronoun "we" and began to explore what the entire team agreed on. The women all agreed with one another that there were significant differences in the treatment of men and women. They stated that while they had formed the company as equals, three men now occupied positions in the executive suite, while the women were given secondary titles. This meant that the men had more decision-making authority and appeared to more readily offer promotions to other men, whereas the women had to be tested for their competency before being considered for a promotion. The women believed that there were other differences that the men simply couldn't see. The men ranged in their opinions, from flat-out disagreement with the women to a weak concession that there might be some inequalities that needed attending to. And while the whole group couldn't agree about the presence of gender bias, through the course of the conversation they came to agree on two very important matters: they all cared about the issue of gender bias, and they were willing to explore their biases within the group. They were also interested in how gender bias in tech companies was being addressed industry-wide.

Enter the third person. Whenever we move to a phase in a conversation where we are sharing indisputable facts, concrete information, research data, or conclusions of studies, we are in *it* territory. And at the right moment, this perspective can be extremely relieving in a conversation. From an objective point of view, everyone could see that men now occupied the highest-ranking positions in the company. Everyone also conceded that although the women had come in as equals, the organization had quickly become stratified according to gender. And there was no disputing that one of the most valuable employees—a woman—had decided to leave the company—an objective reality. At this point, with our help and encouragement, the tone of the conversation changed, and the group began to agree that there were indeed differences in the treatment of men and women that they needed to address. From the perspective of the conversation, everyone was now poised to work together positively on the issue without blame, finger-pointing, or defensiveness.

We praised all the members of the organization for engaging in a difficult series of conversations and for being willing to take positive steps toward creating a different, more equitable culture. We affirmed the willingness of women and men to work together to come up with a shared vision of gender equality. Their ideas included hiring a consultant who would make specific recommendations for fostering positive gender relations, for encouraging diverse leadership and working styles, and for ensuring equal pay and rewards. Most importantly, the team committed to engaging in an ongoing conversation that would advance their shared aspirations and values—conversations that don't create undue animosity or stress but that instead result in greater trust in one another and the ability to take effective action together.

Truth and the Internet

In the internet age we face new, significant challenges related to truth. Ken Wilber says that we are in a "legitimation crisis,"[7] a situation where personal opinions and cultural beliefs are becoming increasingly mismatched with reality. As Wilber says, "A culture that is lying to its members simply cannot move forward for long. And if a culture has 'no truth,' it has no idea when it's lying—and thus it naturally lies as many times as it accidentally tells the truth."[8]

The internet contributes to the legitimation crisis because when appearing online, truth and falsehoods have equal sway. In an article that appeared in *Time* magazine, Joel Stein says that the internet's personality has changed. "Once it was a geek with lofty ideals about the free flow of information. Now, if you need help improving your upload speeds, the web is eager to help with technical details. But if you are struggling with depression, it may goad you into killing yourself." This is referred to as the "disinhibition effect," in which factors like anonymity, invisibility, lack of authority, and not communicating in real time strip away the civility (second person) and the reliability (third person) that society has spent generations building.[9]

Wilber points out that "search engines do not prioritize knowledge in terms of truth, or inclusivity, or values, or depth, or any indexing system at all. . . . Truth plays no role in it."[10] Because this is so, the internet is riddled with fake news, filled with provocative opinion pieces written to attract more clicks,[11] and inhabited by trolls who hide in anonymity and break all norms of civility. As users, we contribute to the confusion about what is real by ignoring sources of information and by failing to cross-check facts and data. We amplify untruths by forwarding and sharing sensational or deeply one-sided stories that we haven't verified. And we uncritically consume media that only echoes our own beliefs.

This crisis in legitimacy can lead to a crisis of meaning. Where collective confidence in meaning and values breaks down, people experience increased anxiety and isolation, not knowing who or what they can trust anymore. So how can we participate in countering this legitimation crisis? Once again, by taking the truth seriously, and by taking a perspective on our perspectives and those of others. We need to see the internet as a forum of perspectives where veracity is not a given, and claims to truth must be shown to be consistent with legitimacy.

First-person opinions have their place, but we should look more deeply into the intention of the person writing the opinion. This means gauging the level of sincerity and evaluating whether the opinion comes directly from someone's personal lived experience or expertise, or whether it is intended to simply illicit outrage, make money as click bait, or gather power through misinformation. We must be discerning because many opinions are born of confusion, ill will, and an impulse toward reactivity. In meditation practice we learn to simply note negative or reactive thoughts and then let them go. We could practice the same way when scrolling down a Facebook page or looking at our Twitter feed. We can learn to be consciously discriminating and take in the "I" perspectives that uplift and encourage us.

Let's then move our attention to the second-person dimension and examine the "we" online (remember "we" is made up of "you" and "me"). We can consciously ask ourselves which groups we share a perspective with and what values that perspective expresses. We can consider who else is included in the perspective and who is left out. We can wonder where the line between "us" and "them" is drawn, and why. We can practice stepping outside our comfort zone and trying on perspectives that are different from our own, if only for a few minutes. When she first moved to the United States, Kim deliberately had different news apps on her smartphone to see how the different headlines were coming through, from the BBC to Fox News to Al Jazeera. Practices like this help us include more points of view and help us find the partial truth in each of them. The more mutually improving, compassionate, and inclusive a set of beliefs and agreements are, the better they are for the whole of us, and the larger the circle of care becomes.

Finally, we should verify what is presented as objective "it" truths we encounter on the web by assessing whether they have been subjected to empirical processes. What science is the assertion based on? Is the research based on sound questions? What studies give the perspective its legitimacy? Who is funding the research? Is it a highly reputable publication like *Science*, which is curated by the American Association for the Advancement of Science, or *Nature*, also a highly reputable source? Or is it a site that mixes politics or religion with science? Publications with peer review processes or editorial boards are far more reliable than those without them. Until internet companies create an editorial function that clearly discerns facts from fiction or opinion, we must rigorously verify truth for ourselves.

We can participate online, as we do in our personal relationships, with more sincerity, goodness, and truth. But we must decide what values matter and be willing to stand up for them. If we are willing to sharpen our own relationship to truth, we are inevitably contributing to more truthfulness for all of us.

THE PRACTICE

1. Choose a story that involves a close friend or partner.
2. Find a friend to listen to you as you explore the three different perspectives of "I," "we," and "it" in telling the story. Or use a journal to do the same thing on your own.
3. Begin with the pronoun "I," and describe your version of events in detail. Experience this way of telling the story as completely true and legitimate.
4. Now tell the story from the third-person perspective of "it," as though it were told by an objective narrator.
5. Finally, tell the story from the perspective of "you" or "we."
6. Explore with your friend what it was like to listen to the story from all three perspectives.

6 *Having a Clear Intention*

Let the power of intention lead the way.

—Sharon Salzberg

Gabriel's alarm went off at 5:15 a.m. *Damn*, he thought, stirring in his bed, *my knees are just as sore as they were yesterday, even after a full night's rest.* He was beginning the third day of a seven-day Zen meditation retreat led by Diane. He wasn't even halfway through the retreat, and he was feeling resistant, exasperated, and exhausted. Overwhelmed by the prospect of more knee pain, he couldn't recall why he had decided to devote a week of his life to sitting still on a cushion.

When he arrived at the meditation hall, he was still preoccupied, confused, and dreading more pain. He forgot to bow to his cushion and just sat down mindlessly. The gong sounded three times, marking the beginning of the sitting period but not the end of his agitation—it persisted throughout the morning as his attention oscillated between drowsiness, a flurry of images and incoherent ideas, and wondering whether the numbness in his foot was related to the pain in his knees. At one point, as he felt his blood circulation being cut off, he actually worried that he might lose his leg from the knee down.

Later, in a one-on-one session with Diane, she asked Gabriel how his sitting was going. After his misery-filled response, Diane said, "May I ask you what intention brought you to this retreat?"

Hearing her question, Gabriel took a spontaneous deep breath and noticed his mind finally beginning to slow down. As Diane held him in her caring yet penetrative presence, his attention finally released him from the grip of his sore knees, freeing him to explore an answer to her question.

"I'm afraid of dying," he said. "Even more than that, I'm afraid of dying without really knowing who I am or what the purpose of my life is."

A few years earlier, when Gabriel was in college, he developed a heart condition, atrial fibrillation, an irregularity in his heartbeat. A diagnosis that turned his world upside down. He had to stop playing basketball. He lost friends as he slowed down the pace of his college life. He couldn't blithely focus on his future as he had before, but now had to care for himself fully in the present. The heart condition forced him into an existential inquiry about who he was and what his values and life purpose were. Consequently, he lost some of his closest friends because they no longer shared the same outlook on life. His encounter with his own mortality had changed him, his intentions, and therefore his world. Exploring Zen practice was a response to this enormous shift in his life.

After a few moments passed, Diane said, "So your intention is to know who you really are and to live your life purpose? In that case, I think you're in the right place."

Returning to his cushion, Gabriel understood again that *intention guides attention*, and that any time he was confused while sitting or overwhelmed by his experience he could reconnect with his intention. While it didn't eliminate the pain, recalling his intention allowed him to settle his mind and sit stably in the here and now. He remembered a quote from Zen master Dogen: "If you cannot find the truth right where you are, where do you expect to find it?"[1]

The origin of the word *intention*, from its Old French and Latin roots, points to two distinct dimensions: the idea of *purpose*, of turning one's attention to this moment; and to *stretch it out over time*. So *to intend* is to cast one's purpose across time and space as if we had a window into the future where we can see our intention fully manifested. By seeing the end state we desire, we can consciously begin to align with that possibility in this very moment. Such is the power of intention. It heightens our awareness, stretches our attention, and guides our development across time and space. And in doing so, the future can be made present.

Intention and Conversation

Having a clear intention will literally help us navigate our conversations when we encounter difficult terrain. To enter a conversation (other than one that is simply social) without an intention is like walking into the wilderness without a compass. And yet we engage in conversations all the time without having one, sometimes without even the vaguest idea of how we would like the conversation to go. Rather than being clear as to what we want, whether it's to assert our truth, to exchange perspectives, to expand our understanding, to learn about another person's life, or to practice listening, we go in blind and end up stumbling all over the place. We lose ourselves in dense, hidden motives ranging from wanting to be right and proving others wrong, to flaunting our expertise and establishing dominance. We become entangled in trying to impress others or trying to self-protect. We aren't prepared for feelings when they crop up, so we ignore or simply cope with them, like wading through unexpected expanses of deserts or boggy swamps. Our important conversations are often rambling, aimless, and in the end, unsatisfying and wearying.

We need a reliable reference point, a North Star if you will, for when the going gets tough. So in our facilitation work, we insist that our groups always agree on a shared intention for a conversation right up-front. Intentions engage the frontal cortex, that part of the brain involved in thinking, planning, and decision-making. It coordinates our thoughts and actions with internal goals and provides us with a healthy focus. As Robert Sapolsky, a Stanford University professor, neuroendocrinologist, and neurobiologist, points out, "The frontal cortex makes you do the harder thing when it's the right thing to do."[2] For example, when anxiety begins to grip the room and we then bring our shared intention to mind, it will often restore relaxation, curiosity, and faith in the process.

Gabriel and Diane organized a workshop that brought together a group of black and white friends to explore and transform their racial dynamics. When putting out the call for the workshop, Gabe explicitly said, "This is a space where everybody, black or white, gay or straight, liberal or conservative, and everyone in-between, must agree to challenge themselves, to grow their heart and communication skills and be accountable to the rest of us. Our intention is to transform our unconscious group dynamics into liberated and mutually affirming relationships."

Typically, most of us engage in conversations about race, gender, politics, or religion not to grow our heart, but to confirm our own personal beliefs and perceptions, including proving others wrong. Group identity and loyalty to our own tribe has far more influence on what we think, believe, and say than we would like to admit. In this workshop, Gabe deliberately formulated the intention to have conversations that were fresh and revealing, and that gave everyone a chance to grow their skill set. To meet these aims, everyone had to buy into the shared intention. Leaders in human development research assert that individual adults can grow and develop new capacities indefinitely: cognitive, emotional, moral, and even one's sense of self.[3] And this personal growth can translate to broader cultural change, greater political skillfulness, better leadership, and more effective activism.

Gabe interviewed each person who answered the invitation. He wanted to make sure that their intentions and desires were aligned with those of the workshop. After talking with some potential participants it became clear that the workshop was not appropriate for them. Some were more interested in conversations regarding politics or activism; others wanted to do healing rather than relationship work. Some potential participants felt that the premise that we are *all* responsible for transforming relationships was faulty since some identity groups have obviously dominated and abused others. But Gabe was clear about the purpose of the conversation he convened. The clarity of his intention helped his friends determine if it was the right conversation for them. There are all kinds of useful conversations, but they may have very different intentions, and therefore outcomes.

An explicit shared intention serves like a cell membrane for conversation. It includes those who share the intention and excludes those who don't. This is especially important at a time when in many settings we place a premium on inclusion. We may feel that we need to admit anyone who wants to participate in the conversation, but mixed intentions create mixed results. When people have different purposes and outcomes in mind, conversation can grind to a halt. But with a clear direction, when people have primed their frontal cortex to do the hard thing when it's the right thing to do, conversations can evolve into creative, energized experiences, where more and more perspectives can come to light.

Resistance, Opposition, and Receptivity

An intention does more than create a positive direction; it also creates resistance and opposition. Have you ever set a New Year's intention and the first thing you notice is how much you resist it? Have you ever noticed when you commit to a discipline how many of your habits that are precisely the opposite come fully into view? For example, if we intend to listen, we'll begin to notice all the ways that we simply don't want to. If we intend to hold multiple points of view, we'll notice all the times we collapse into one solid, unyielding perspective. The intention to go *up* highlights the experience of going *down*; our desire for *this* points out how often we do *that* instead.

But resistance is extremely good news because opposition points to exactly the times, places, and patterns that we need to work with in order to grow our skills. Practice takes time; it requires repetition, and encountering obstacles is intrinsic to our growth and skill-building.[4] Resistance functions like gravity, creating drag on our systems, and overcoming it requires galvanizing strength, ingenuity, and determination. Without resistance, our new habits we're trying to establish don't become as strong and durable. So working with intention necessarily includes encountering resistance and dealing with opposition. Our mistakes and failures are golden opportunities to slow down, examine the moment, and look for alternative responses.

For example, Anthony, an African American participant in the training, shared with the group one of his greatest frustrations about white people: "You all unwittingly promote institutional oppression by enjoying its benefits while being blind to how those very same benefits are not extended equally to people of color. For instance, in my university context, the hiring is often done by committees of people in leadership, all of whom are white. So it's no surprise that they hire more white people. And then they wonder why we don't have more diversity in our department." He went on: "I want a white ally who really gets this!"

His passion and intensity had an enormous impact on the room. After a few moments of letting his message sink in, we asked for a white participant to reflect what he or she had heard Anthony say. Lizzie raised her hand and very deliberately repeated what she had heard: "White people, including myself, enjoy the benefits of our systems and institutions while failing to notice how the benefits exclude people of color." She mirrored his energy and his frustrations.

She continued: "I've done a lot of work on myself, and there is a lot more work I need to do around my blind spots. But here's what I've come to recognize about how I perpetuate white supremacy through the institutions I participate with." She then briefly shared some poignant examples that showed that she understood first hand his point of view. She also shared the efforts she is undertaking personally to account for the impact of her actions.

"Yeah, yeah, that's fine, but my colleagues don't see it, and it drives me crazy!" Anthony protested. Now, it's important to note that the shared intention of this workshop was to *deepen our connection to one another through our differences.*

"Hold on" Diane said, jumping into the interaction. "Anthony, you just asked for a white ally who shares your understanding, but I didn't see you take in what Lizzie just said. How did you hear her? Did her message have any impact on you?"

Anthony seemed startled. He paused, looking back at Lizzie. It was a poignant moment to see him take her in, as if for the first time.

"Yes," he said, "totally. Thank you for that, Lizzie. Wow. I feel way more relaxed knowing you see this, too." He reflected further. "It's crazy that I missed that connection, Lizzie. I think I'm so accustomed to being the only black man on my team, where I'm always the sole person pointing out how institutions perpetuate this shit. And so I failed to listen to what you were saying because I was just gearing up to make my point again."

It was a small but intimate moment. Anthony's role as an advocate, which was brave and difficult, actually took over in his conversation with Lizzie and prevented him from forging a connection with an ally he wanted. His takeaway from the weekend was that while in his activist mode he still needs to maintain an openness to receiving potential allies and connections, who may be closer than he thinks.

An intentional conversation, particularly one focused on the growth of our skills, is geared to disrupt our habitual and reactive patterns so that new perceptions, insights, and skills can come in. Gabe's intention was to engage differences and to challenge conditioned patterns and biased views so that everyone in his group could genuinely become one another's allies. His conversation was meant to free everyone to care more deeply about one another and for their work together.

Mutual intentions create powerful experiences. Gabriel's workshop participants experienced a way of being with themselves and others that they had been longing for. Inevitably, there came a moment when they realized that the workshop would end, and they would return to the many mixed intentions of everyday life. Gabriel joked with the participants: "Yeah, when you walk into Starbucks they won't share our intention, and they won't be using our ground rules. Neither will the other drivers on the freeway. Or the people dealing with your credit card or tech problem. Or the passenger sitting next to you on the airplane. Or perhaps some of your colleagues at the university. But your individual intention will affect and shape the way *you* show up, and that is the greatest power you have. And the freedom, intimacy, and camaraderie that you thought could never be created or sustained in the real world will simply become who you are. And that change is the best contribution you can make to the world."

THE PRACTICE

1. The next time you enter into a casual conversation, take a moment to quietly form an intention.
2. At several points during the conversation, revisit that intention and allow it to influence your contribution. Notice whether having a clear intention changed your experience.

1 Conversation Essentials

Rumi says there are three ways to talk to God. Through meditation, through prayer, and through conversation.

—Coleman Barks

In our increasingly interconnected world, the sheer volume of conversations stretching across the planet is spectacular. Like virtual wires encircling and lighting up the globe, conversations enliven us, orient us, and connect us. Some are bright and fleeting. Others maintain a steady glow over a lifetime, giving warmth, color, and continuity to our relationships. A few are sparky and fractious, while some provide powerful, light-filled connections with loved ones far away. Some provide direct contact with complete strangers, whose viewpoints can be wildly unfamiliar and far-fetched, such that sometimes we just need to unplug.

But virtual conversations aren't quite enough. People increasingly bemoan the loss of real human interaction because we rely so much on technology rather than face-to-face contact. Our lives and schedules are often so jammed that we fail to slow down and really talk. When we do engage, we tend to move quickly, discussing past and future but missing the full presence and spontaneity of this very moment. So in this virtual, fast-paced culture, if we want direct contact, intimacy, and meaningful conversation, we must turn our attention toward it, value it, and cultivate it.

As a starting point we may wonder that with so much opportunity for conversation and such a multiplicity of identities, cultural contexts, and personal preferences, what makes for a good conversation, one that genuinely satisfies? How do we engage in constructive, dynamic exchanges that include our differences, *especially* when something important is at stake? Shared intention is a must. In addition, the use of ground rules or guiding principles helps us find direction when the territory feels challenging or unfamiliar. When conversations are anxiety-provoking or divisive, ground rules or guiding principles are essential to success. Six that we have found very helpful[1] are:

1. Be for each other.
2. Listen well.
3. Talk straight.
4. Give support and challenge.
5. Use praise.
6. Keep agreements.

I. Be for Each Other

Recently, Diane was in a late-night conversation at a conference, discussing Integral Theory and Ken Wilber's work. She was sitting with a couple of friends in a dorm room when an Integral colleague and his friend showed up at the door. She invited them in, and they immediately found seats and a place in the conversation. It was lively and energized. Her colleague had a lot of perspectives to share, and the new person, too, was fully present and engaged. Perhaps because he was new to the group, the newcomer listened intently.

At a certain point, Diane and her Integral colleague began to argue about some of the fine points of the theory, or maybe they disagreed about one of Wilber's meanings—who knows, it doesn't really matter. The conversation became a little more strained, with traces of struggle and disagreement. Diane began to feel irritated and somewhat threatened by her colleague's style. He continued to promote his perspective in a way that made her feel dominated by him. Now she was fully on the defensive and, knowing her, the offensive as well. While this went on, the newcomer sat perfectly at ease and present, even with the changing tone of the discourse.

Finally, she'd had enough. She told her colleague that she had lost interest in the conversation because they were arguing instead of exploring. She was vehement and resolute in her critique. Her colleague was initially defensive and then apologetic. But shortly thereafter he reasserted himself. She was provoked once again and pointed the problem out once again. He retreated, but not for long. He went back to reiterating his original point; she protested again. They went back and forth for another twenty minutes or so like this. All the while the newcomer stayed fully present, engaged, and remarkably nonjudgmental.

She was impressed by the newcomer's countenance. When the conflict was finally resolved and Diane and her colleague were in harmony again, she turned her attention to the newcomer. "I'm impressed by how present you were with us—how you maintained your interest, and how much you seemed to trust our struggle." He politely thanked her.

The newcomer's name was Lloyd Fickett, and he introduced Diane to the ground rules he writes about in his work *The Collaborative Way: A Story about Engaging the Mind and Spirit of a Company*.[2] There is tremendous overlap in lists of ground rules that people use in group work settings and meetings, but his first ground rule, *be for each other*, was one that Diane had never encountered before. She realized that this commitment from him was exactly what she had appreciated that night in the dorm. She had recognized that he was calm, present, and free of judgment about her conflict with her colleague. But now she understood that he was literally "for" her, just as he was "for" her Integral colleague. And she felt it.

Being for each other means remembering, even when we don't feel it, that we want the best for other people. Our differences can create feelings of separation, and the fight-or-flight response deepens our anxiety. When we are triggered, the felt sense in the body is that something is wrong, and usually that someone is "bad." In a situation like that, it's very easy to feel that we are no longer colleagues, friends, or allies. Later, when we calm down, the negative feelings recede and positive ones return. Being for each other serves as a cognitive cue that can literally help us stay connected to others through the ups and downs of difficult conversations. The more we use it, the easier it is to remember our goodwill toward others and the value of our bonds.

This is more challenging with people with whom we are less familiar or those with whom we have significant conflicts. In *Nonviolent Communication: A Language of Life*, psychologist, mediator, and teacher Marshall Rosenberg describes how he participated in a mediated conflict in the Middle East/West Asia that seemed completely intractable.[3] When the parties met together for the first time, the leaders were furious, each accusing the other side of inciting violence. Through careful and sensitive questioning by the facilitators, they were able to establish that both sides genuinely sought safety and peace so that their children and future generations did not have to live in fear of murder or violence.[4] In this they shared the same wish, and it was something they could work toward together. Here, the Dalai Lama's advice is helpful: "All others' desires are the same as mine. Every being wants happiness and does not want suffering."[5] All people want to be heard, to feel respected and valued. Remembering this, it's easy to practice being for each other.

2. Listen Well

If we could make only one suggestion for improving our conversations about difference, it would be to insist that everyone practice reflective listening skills.[6] Reflective listening is simple and involves just two steps: First, the listener opens up to hear and fully receive the speaker's message. Second, the listener repeats the message back to the speaker to confirm that it was understood accurately. This is *listen well*, a very simple skill, and it is golden. Unfortunately, we tend not to do it.

Why don't we use this simple technique more often? Maybe we feel awkward parroting other people's remarks, or perhaps we worry we will come off as pretentious, semitherapeutic, or patronizing. Or we might be avoiding any move that signals agreement. Sometimes it backfires, and people react negatively to the reflections. Nonetheless, when we are sincere and use the technique to genuinely give others the experience that they have been heard, it's amazing how well it works. Take this example:

We assisted two women who worked for a small nonprofit. One was the administrator of the organization who occupied various roles. The younger of the two, who had a strong business background, was hired to assist the administrator. They had an energized and creative relationship, working autonomously at home on their computers, with short bursts of direct collaboration on reports, projects, and financials.

The stress emerged when the administrator, who felt they were falling behind on some tasks, asked to put more routines in place. To her surprise, her younger colleague was offended by her request. It seemed that a generational difference had come between them. The administrator had worked in more conventional organizations during her career, and she was used to showing up at the office, coordinating her work, and scheduling meetings. The younger colleague had spent most of her life as a consultant or contractor and always worked according to her own schedule. She interpreted the request to coordinate their work and meet more often as a criticism about the quality of her work.

The rapport between them quickly turned to alienation, and so they sought help from us to resolve their dispute. When we met in person they were cordial, but also tense. They reluctantly began talking, each sharing her perceptions. But after twenty minutes or so, talking hadn't helped them become any more open or relaxed. So we asked them to each take time to reflect on what they actually heard the other saying. When they began to offer feedback on each other's messages, the felt sense between them changed immediately. The warmth and care they had previously enjoyed seemed to return, along with their sense of humor. Suddenly, friendship emerged again, even some tenderness, along with a willingness on both their parts to reset their relationship.

The reflective listening had an energetic impact on them. By taking time to thoroughly receive the message of the other, the women were able to reestablish sameness, connection, and rapport. And as they created room for each other's perspective, their empathy had a soothing effect. Most importantly, they gave each other the direct experience of being heard, which is always an incredible relief. They were able to put their guard down and allow the mutual appreciation between them to return.

Reflective listening is an art that takes some practice. We must empty our mind, be present to the other person, and relax. It's important to repeat the message clearly without distorting it. It also helps to pay attention to the emotional tone and to include that. A few follow-up questions like "Did I understand you correctly?" or "Is there something else you want to add?" shows one's curiosity and open mind, and invites the speaker to affirm or clarify their true meaning.

3. Talk Straight

Talk straight is a ground rule that encourages us to speak our truth simply and straightforwardly. Easy, right? We just need to be clear about what it is we want to say and then say it. But our messages often become mixed, distorted, or unskillful in all kinds of ways. Usually it's some form of anxiety that creates the problem. This is particularly true in the domain of conversations related to social justice, identity, or power dynamics. We can get quite caught up in our own viewpoint and come off as dogmatic or self-righteous. Or we can become tentative or insecure, trying to say just the right thing, compulsively avoiding mistakes. Or we can overdo our politically correct demands so that everyone loses the inspiration to engage any further—it simply isn't worth the risk or discomfort.

Talking straight is easier when we remember how much we appreciate it when others talk straight to us. For example, after writing the first chapter of this book regarding the evolution of human culture, Diane sent it to Greg Thomas, a friend and fellow Integralist who is a writer, editor, and public speaker in New York City.[7] Greg writes about culture, race, and democratic life, and especially about jazz in American culture. He is definitely someone whose perspective we valued when writing about the challenges of talking about race and other such charged topics.

In his note back, Greg said he appreciated the chapter overall but gave Diane the feedback that it overrelied on the tired victim-oppressor storyline. He said that he believes, along with the literary critics Ralph Ellison and Albert Murray, and others, that this narrative is far too simplistic and inadequate because it fails to acknowledge the tremendous resilience and resourcefulness that emerges when people encounter adversity. "Forgive my exasperation," Greg said, "but there is an intellectual tradition that confronted identity politics decades ago, and yet we are still shackled by it!"

Damn, Diane thought, reading his note. *I feel you, Greg.*

Diane had asked him what he thought, and he straight-up told her. Anytime you ask for feedback you are asking for people to talk straight. So you had better be prepared to take it in and at least think it over a bit. Greg was clear in his feedback; he was straightforward, and he took responsibility for his own emotions. He was clearly frustrated with the direction of our writing in that section, but we genuinely appreciated his willingness to give us his opinion, even if it wasn't a rave review. Furthermore—and this is important—he had confidence in Diane's ability to hear him out. We have to trust that when we are direct, others have the ego strength to hear our message. Whether they agree with us or not is another matter. Always remember that listening doesn't equal agreement. In this instance, we did make some revisions to include Greg's feedback.

Some part of this ground rule is culturally determined. In other words, for some groups it would always be impolite to be so direct. But within the work we do, this ground rule flows very naturally out of the previous ground rules, *be for each other* and *listen well*. In talking straight, we invite conversation participants to orient most of their communications from the first-person perspective. This means using "I messages,"[8] as in "I think that . . ." or "I feel that . . ." or "I want this . . ." or "I will do this . . ." The reason for this is that "I messages" convey only what is true for the individual. They don't imply big empirical truths that need to be verified. They don't require us to speak on behalf of our group. They don't require agreement from those listening. They capture our own direct experience, our personal perceptions, and in doing so they acknowledge that our "I" truths are modest, manageable, and exist in relation to other relevant truths. This is what makes conversation interesting and exciting—we don't see things the same way.

Of course, talking straight takes practice. As we said earlier, sometimes our early attempts are full of anxiety, so it takes a little courage to be forthcoming about our views and then to be available to receive the feedback or disagreement that inevitably results. We must learn to clarify our messages, freeing them from traces of aggression and negative judgments, and this takes time and practice to accomplish. But this ground rule encourages us to be brave, to take risks by being ourselves, and to learn from experience. Practicing being direct and clear, we learn to trust ourselves and in turn, to trust others. Eventually, we find out how to hear, respect, and integrate our differences.

4. Give Support and Challenge

In many of our conversations today there is a tremendous amount of emphasis placed on safety. Safety is a way to describe an atmosphere of sameness, of mutual support, belonging, or rapport between group members. Group safety also conveys dependability, trust, and absence of threat. When we feel safe, we perform better, take more risks, and are willing to make mistakes.[9] We can create safety in our groups by giving everyone a voice, being for each other, using listening skills, asking questions, and extending goodwill.

But have you ever belonged to a group that was so safe and supportive that it lacked energy? Or one that valued safety so much that the purpose of the group became secondary to a preoccupation with triggers, microaggressions, or spotlighting anything that seemed unsafe? Or one that professed to value tolerance in such a way that it became wildly intolerant? Or one in which people protect other members of the group, even when they don't seem to want or need protection? When cultivated with skill and proportionality, safety creates the conditions for challenging in a healthy way, and this is what it means to follow the fourth ground rule, *give support and challenge.*

Challenges keep groups exciting, dynamic, and creative, and they help people learn and grow. When we challenge one another, we expand our perspectives and integrate new information, or we tolerate the creative tension of our differences. Have you ever learned or accomplished anything that didn't involve consistent challenges? Without them, we experience stagnation, inertia, boredom, and irritability. But in a healthy, dynamic group, people learn to offer challenges in the form of questions, contrasting perspectives, and critiques, with the right level of intensity, timing, and frequency to keep things lively and exciting. If we are interested in growth and learning, we must find just the right combination of these two qualities: support and challenge.

5. Offer Praise

We always suggest the ground rule *offer praise.* Within the context of conversation there are many moments where we can express appreciation. We could give a little shout-out to a person's insight, or comment on the poignancy of a story, or admire someone's listening skills. It's very supportive to others in conversation to specifically note actions that contribute to a good conversation, but so often we don't.

Praise is a lofty word, a little old-fashioned, somewhat saccharine, with religious overtones. People fear that if they agree to offer praise as a ground rule it will become an unnecessary obligation, like going to church. Or it could become meaningless if we require it, like when everyone in the class gets a trophy just for being there. Or it could be confused with an anxious, unspoken need for approval and create more anxiety in the room. Some participants would prefer to skip the praise part altogether and just appreciate one another occasionally, or give positive feedback every once in a while. But we contend that offering praise is perfect for all of these reasons. We use it because it asks perhaps a little too much, and this stretches us to give it; because it creates a habit of recognizing good work and goodwill; and because it heightens our habit of appreciating others for their perseverance, hard work, unique talents, and their ability to sustain commitments.

Our friend Julia is a kind, rare person whose nuanced, thinking mind is inextricable from the workings of her truly devotional heart. Julia is also an expert in praise. She went to Catholic schools when she was young, and she recalls how the nuns never praised her or anybody else for that matter. Instead, she was taught to scrub floors, wash windows, and keep it to herself—in other words, to maintain the "spirit of quiet."

But at night, all by herself in her bed, she would break the rules of the convent and read a writer beloved by her, French paleontologist and mystic Pierre Teilhard de Chardin. In *Hymn of the Universe* he assured her that all creations are worthy of praise, with no exceptions, including her.[10] While the nuns might critique her every move, the secret teachings she received from de Chardin confirmed that everything and everyone is praiseworthy because everything and everyone is God.

Julia also read Dante's *Divine Comedy* without permission from the nuns. In the *Paradiso*, the third volume of this epic work, Dante sets forward a vision of heaven in which the beings in the higher realms are more capable of knowing and loving God and therefore more filled with his glory. These domains are infused with the ceaseless activity of angels whose primary purpose is to praise. They praise with all the force of their angelic will and mirror the Divine:

The Eternal Goodness that divides Itself
into these countless mirrors that reflect Itself, remaining One,
as It was always.[11]

Dante's view is that praise is the highest form of human expression, that it reflects eternal goodness and divine unity. Praise is supremely beneficial as a practice in all conversations because it enhances connection, highlights uniqueness, and polishes our deep commonality. By praising we affirm the beautiful, intrinsic value of our work and relationships; we encourage commitment and generosity; and we actively appreciate our basic goodness.

6. Keep Agreements

Our final suggestion is that we agree to uphold these ground rules and keep any other agreements we make. *Keeping agreements* is essential to all good conversation and the trust it requires. Agreements are a form of truth and create a firm foundation for every conversation. Even though we may have serious differences in our perspectives, viewpoints, and strategies, agreeing on a shared intention or a set of ground rules creates a reliable basis for all further agreements.

Employing these ground rules has been tremendously supportive of our ability to hold difficult conversations. In facilitated settings it is certainly worth articulating these clearly and explicitly at the outset. In personal, informal encounters with family, peers, or colleagues they can also be used. When entering tricky conversational territory it can be helpful to suggest a ground rule or two. For example, "I really want to talk about this. Can we agree to pause and reflect what we hear each other say?" or "This topic is often stressful to discuss. Can we agree that we will still be for each other when our conversation is over?" or "I want you to know from the outset that I might challenge your opinion, but I value our differences."

There are moments in the course of a conversation when we have to interrupt and remind people of these ground rules. When hostility emerges in people's speech, we stop and reflect that we agreed to *be for each other*. When excitement takes over and the pace of conversation is fast and furious, we ask people to slow down and *listen well*. When participants in a conversation are scared, tentative, or sending mixed messages, we encourage them to *talk straight* and share what's really on their minds. When people are anxiety-ridden, we bring forward *support*; and when they are listless, distracted, or overly polite, we invite *challenge* into the room. And we are constantly reminding participants to *offer praise* because it's just straight-up good for everyone. These agreements are simple yet profound. They demand little but deliver a ton. Please give them a go. You'd be surprised how much they help.

THE PRACTICE

1. Try out this set of ground rules and see how they work for you.
2. Explore other ground rules, and make up your own.

8 *Hidden Biases*

We don't see things as they are, we see them as we are.
—attributed to the Talmud

In learning to talk about our differences, we notice that we all have blind spots.[1] That is, we have hidden biases that influence our behavior, particularly related to how we see and interact with people from other groups. They are invisible to us, but like a black hole in space, if we are open to the idea that they exist, we may come to learn about them and eventually shine a light their way.

Diane recalls having her eyes opened to up-close and personal experiences of racism by a colleague and friend, Karen, who is black. They worked together in Utah in the nineties when there was a big push in that state to address racial and ethnic fairness in the justice system. Karen and Diane were involved in training court employees about the value of diversity and challenging forms of racism within the criminal justice system. The training was required of certain groups of court employees, and anyone who has ever participated in mandatory training knows how difficult it is to work with an audience whose boss has told them that they have to spend a day in a training session.

Karen and Diane worked as a team. Rather than delivering lifeless platitudes about the obligations of the courts and how people should be treated, they sought to establish rapport with their reluctant groups, engaging them in real, sometimes risky conversation. They tried to foster an atmosphere of genuine inquiry in which participants could explore the values of fairness and equal treatment that the justice system promises, while at the same time taking a closer look at their own prejudices and the biased behaviors they had witnessed or experienced from others.

Karen easily created rapport with the group, and she naturally shared some of her own experiences growing up as a black woman in Utah, an overwhelmingly white state. As she taught the curriculum and engaged participants in conversations about their views, she deftly revealed her own encounters with prejudice and how she learned to cope with them. She described incidents that were common in her life, incidents that Diane recognized were not common in hers, like being randomly followed by a security guard in a department store, or being pulled over by police for no apparent reason, or not feeling free to walk onto a property to inquire about a house that is for sale, or sitting on a bus with two empty seats on either side of you when the rest of the bus is full.

Karen also recalled being the object of racial slurs, unspoken hostility, and even hatred from people she had never met before. She wove her stories and anecdotes in a way that allowed the group to see how she was subjected to racism almost every time she walked out her front door. Karen wasn't required to share herself in this way; some people feel it's not the job of people of color to educate white people. But Karen took the opportunity provided by the courts to open a window onto her world. By the end of the training, the group was no longer reluctant, but engaged. Everyone empathized, feeling the exhaustion, pain, and mistrust that features in the everyday lives of people of color.

Diane's biggest takeaway from the training was a lesson about herself. Growing up, it was apparent to her that whites were not innately superior to other groups. But she had failed to really see, in vivid detail, the world through the eyes of a person of color—how relentless the experience of racism is; how it ranges in scale from the tiniest mean glance to mass incarceration.[2] How it isn't limited to our individual attitudes, but is sustained through our interpersonal habits as well as institutions like the court and prison systems. How it is so pervasive that for a well-meaning white person like Diane to see it clearly, she must look through the eyes of someone who lives it every day.[3]

Diane also learned that like the people in her training, she had to shed light on her own blind spots. She had to reflect on why, in the third grade, her Diné (i.e., Navajo) classmate refused to stand for the Pledge of Allegiance, and that no one ever acknowledged or even mentioned the decimation of his Native American culture. She had to look at how, in the sixth grade, she was very good friends with three girls of Mexican heritage, but in seventh grade their friendships literally dissolved as she moved into a group of all-white friends. This happened without anyone saying a word. She became an officer in student government with other white students, while none of her Latina friends did. Diane had to think later about why that happened, and why she never paid attention to it at the time. She had to recall how in high school her father was always more vigilant when she danced with a black friend or was asked out by somebody with brown skin, something he never did when she went out with white boys. She saw in retrospect that she simply tolerated her father's ethnocentrism without ever questioning him.

These were all hidden biases, meaning she couldn't see them. Like the other white kids, she was inured to the assumptions of white culture that had shaped her perceptions, afforded her privileges not shared by her friends of color, and even dictated her relationships. Only over time was she able to glimpse her biases and begin to challenge the implicit assumption all around her that white people belonged on top—basically, white supremacy.

So, she decided to open her mind and drop her preconceptions, to ask questions and listen, even when what she heard or felt was uncomfortable. She learned to calm herself when she felt defensive so she could listen better, and to tolerate feeling that she had done something wrong.

She also learned that conversation that builds real relationships with people who are different helps us see one another as full human beings, and not as the flat, one-dimensional stereotypes we hold in our mind. And maybe most importantly, she came to understand the harm caused by these implicit patterns of discrimination, and find her own ways to challenge them.

Implicit Biases in Systems

Michael D. Zimmerman is Diane's husband. He was a justice on the Utah Supreme Court for sixteen years. When he was chief justice, Michael helped establish the Task Force on Racial and Ethnic Fairness within the criminal justice system. The task force pulled together people working throughout the system, from police officers, to prosecutors, judges, and prison officials. The task force also included representatives from the wider community, including social workers and educators. They examined the criminal justice process from beginning to end, locating the points of bias against people of color.

Our criminal justice system has a goal of equal treatment of all people under the law. When you ask most people working within the system whether they believe it honors that goal, they will strongly agree that it does. They would also say that as employees in the system, they are not biased but work diligently to be fair. But statistical analysis shows that at each point in the criminal justice system where individual discretion is exercised, from stops and arrests, to granting and fixing bail amounts, to determining what crimes to charge, to plea bargaining, to convictions, to sentencing, to granting parole or revoking it, people of color are treated more harshly. The cumulative effect of each of these decisions is that people of color are convicted and incarcerated in numbers highly disproportionate to the population as a whole. This confirms the perception of people in communities of color that they are, indeed, subject to unfair treatment.[4]

While some of this disproportion may be due to other factors, recent research makes it clear that implicit bias is at work on the part of the decision-makers.[5] And within a system as elaborate as criminal justice, there is a complexity to this problem that amounts to *structural oppression*—the cumulative and compounding effects of institutions and policies that systematically privilege white people and disadvantage people of color. Because of how pervasive and entrenched the bias is, it will never be transformed if we simply look to individuals to become aware of their own internal biases. Instead, it must be addressed on a systemic level through a range of interventions, such as diverse hiring practices, use of technology in policing, improvements in jury-pool representation, adequate interpreters in the courts, and gathering of accurate data to provide better feedback to law enforcement, prosecutors, and court personnel.[6]

Conversations about Blind Spots

Social change occurs through efforts made in our individual understanding, in initiatives applied in our systems, and within the context of our relationships. Gabe relates two stories about bias that he learned through his relationships with women. The first happened when he was in junior high school, and the second when he was in college. In both cases the bias was brought to his attention by someone he valued. These encounters can be embarrassing, painful, or awkward because nobody likes having their blind spots pointed out. At the same time, in an atmosphere of love and caring, it's one of the favors we can do for one another.

It was an ordinary early morning getting ready for school. Gabe and Leo, his younger brother, sat at the kitchen table like junior high boys do, moaning and groaning about having to get up early, partly out of protest and partly just to be funny. The kitchen was busy with activity as Gabe's mom and dad prepared breakfast and snacks for school and bustled around taking care of other details for the day.

Earlier in the week, Gabe had encountered a new experience. He had been hearing his friends whisper and joke about certain girls: "Hmm, I bet she's PMSing . . ." The boys laughed, snickered, and got a lot of pleasure from this. Gabe felt cool being on the inside of this new tease, but to be honest, he wasn't exactly sure what PMS was. He would have asked somebody but was afraid he would be the next one everyone laughed at, so he passed. He had, however, pieced together that the term was thrown out whenever a girl showed the slightest irritability. By the end of the school week, as far as he could tell, all the girls had PMSed at least a couple of times.

During this busy morning of getting ready, Gabe's mom and dad had a quick, heated back-and-forth about a miscommunication over logistics. Gabe seized the opportunity to demo his new understanding and said very loudly and dramatically, "Ha! Mom must be PMSing!" Gabe's dad and mom immediately stopped the banter between them and simultaneously turned to bear down on Gabe. It's safe to say that his joke did not go over well.

"What did you say?" his dad replied, glaring.

His mom chimed in, "What did you say? Do you even know what you said?" She was incredulous.

Gabe froze. He had expected to have some fun with his parents, and instead he was getting a huge reprimand. He still wasn't sure exactly why, so he sputtered something about friends at school, kidding around, and PMS. Seeing her young son's predicament, his mom switched her tone from that of an outraged woman to an understanding mother.

"You probably don't know this yet, Gabe," she said, "but young women have something called a menstrual cycle or period. We can talk more about it later. But for right now, PMS refers to premenstrual syndrome. These are symptoms that occur around the time of the period. Just know that sometimes we can become irritable, tired, or moody. But every woman or girl is different, and not everyone becomes more testy or irritable. And every moment of irritability doesn't have to do with having a period. I'm annoyed this morning, but I'm not PMSing. I'm just annoyed. The important point is that having a period is natural to being a girl, and not something to be teased about."

This was the first time that Gabe was schooled about the differences between boys and girls, men and women, and it was the first time that he recognized that his friends were practicing put-downs of girls. His parents made it painfully clear that he was not to tease girls for being different from boys. He says this was the beginning of becoming an ally to women.

Another wake-up came later in Gabe's life. This time he was at an outdoor coffee shop, between classes at Stanford. He was sitting with a good friend, talking over events from the weekend. It was a beautiful spring day. The woman he was with was also beautiful in Gabe's eyes, and he admits, in retrospect, to checking her out while they were talking—meaning he was looking at her breasts.

"Eyes up here, please," she said.

Gabe was completely caught off guard.

His friend carefully redirected his gaze from her breasts by pointing back up to her eyes. She was, as Gabe recalls, gentle, somewhat amused, but also very firm. He was painfully and deeply embarrassed. And he was genuinely taken aback because he wasn't fully aware at the time that he had been looking at her breasts.

Gabe walked back to his dorm alone, chagrinned, and highly aware of how he was seeing the other students around him. He allowed his attention to move between the forms of men and women. Being a straight man, he felt utterly neutral toward the bodies of men. He looked at them with one glance, and he remembers thinking *just a dude*. But when he turned his attention to women, everything changed. The experience was profound, potent, and primitive. He literally zeroed in on their body parts: legs, butt, breasts. The best way to describe his experience, he says, was "They weren't women. They were a set of breasts walking toward me, or a pair of legs walking away."

The crude term *piece of ass* became real to him that day. For the first time he understood what objectifying women meant. And he saw how his desire to sleep with them framed and filtered his interactions with them. Most importantly, his friend's willingness to explicitly redirect his gaze made him aware that women experienced this objectification and didn't necessarily like it. This was the first time that he had ever considered its impact on them. Even though it originated from deep in his male biology,

Gabe's sexualization and objectification of women was a form of a blind spot. So, he decided to see if he could change his automatic responses.

First, he began to practice how he looked at others. When he saw women, he would widen his lens and intentionally take in the whole female form, just as he did men's bodies. When interacting with his women friends he focused intently on what they were saying in conversation, completely letting go of his desire to be with them sexually. Later he decided to take a whole year off from pursuing women altogether. During that time he turned down anyone who made advances toward him. He wanted to get clear on this inherent blind spot and discover a way to connect with women beyond engaging them solely for his own pleasure. He wanted to discover deeper, more nourishing forms of intimacy, and fuller, more sustained experiences of connection.

Gabe's experiment demonstrates that we can all learn to relate to one another in more authentic ways, taking the other's experience into account. Fully entering the subjective world of one another is compassion. When men and women and all people of diverse gender identity do this, we will all have become one another's allies.

We All Have Blind Spots

Research suggests that everyone has blind spots and hidden biases. It seems to be a product of the efficiency of our mind in creating categories and assigning meaning.[7] Blind spots can be big or small, but regardless, they always distort our perceptions. Acknowledging their existence helps us recognize that our perspectives have built-in limits; that they are true and partial, and there is far more to reality than what we see. Allowing others to point them out to us can be part of fresh and real relationships. How else will we glimpse them? In the process, we become a little more humble, with a little more space in our mind to learn and grow. But it can be embarrassing to stumble on even a small one. But this one, in hindsight, is obvious:

At a gathering of international development practitioners, Kim remembers a conversation in which a comment revealed a blind spot of hers. Talking to a woman from Colombia about her peace-building research work, Kim made reference to an organization in Brazil, assuming that the Colombian woman would know what she was talking about. There was an awkward pause, and then a slightly curt response from the Colombian woman. Kim got the message: Latin America is a big place, and just because you live in one country doesn't mean that you necessarily know anything about what's happening on the other side of the continent.

Kim later reflected on the incident rather sheepishly because she herself has often been in the shadow of the same blind spot. She has been greeted with *Konnichiwa*, a Japanese greeting meaning "Good day," even though she is Chinese. She has also been asked to explain food from different countries across Southeast Asia. Despite those experiences, she realized that she had fallen into the exact same pattern with the woman from Columbia. It was a small moment with a big impact, and Kim took the encounter as an opportunity for humility, a chance to check her assumptions, especially in relation to different cultural contexts. It strengthened her desire to remain curious and to connect with new and different people with greater intentionality.

An Unbiased Mind

Of course, we all have biases, preferences, and prejudices. We see the world through the filters of our likes and dislikes, our hopes and fears. Some of our biases are just the efficiency of our brain, like seeing fire and knowing it's hot. And some are handed off to us by our family, culture, or context, and influence the way we see the world and others. Our prejudices are usually not based on reason or first hand experience and are often so deep that we literally can't see them.

But we can *learn* to see them, particularly if we let other people point them out to us, and we can also learn to relinquish them because our mind, in its essential nature, is naturally free of them. Sometimes we are instructed to wipe the mirror of our mind clean through meditation; other times we are told to simply see the inherent nature of our mind, free of biases and fixed views.

As one Zen master said,

The Great Way is not difficult for those
who have no preferences.
When love and hate are both absent,
everything becomes clear and undisguised.
Make the smallest distinction, however,
and heaven and earth are set infinitely apart.[8]

The Zen master here is referring not to our thinking mind, which holds endless views and ideas about the world and its people, but to our open awareness. Awareness simply perceives things as they are now, without interpretations, categories, or evaluations. It is not the mind that talks to itself like a twenty-four-hour news channel about what it likes or dislikes, what it wants, or what it's afraid of. It just notices things as they are right now. It's like when Galileo looked up at the night sky and rather than seeing a medieval model of fixed celestial spheres, he saw the sky as it actually was—a system of planets moving around the sun.

Meditation is a practice that helps us settle the mind, unwinding our tendency to create categories of right and wrong, for and against. Sitting quietly upright, things are simply as they are, here and now. The mind returns to its original state—open, empty, free of egoic compulsions and fixed identity. In time, this cultivation of open awareness contributes to more flexibility of the mind and a concurrent ability to include more perspectives. Our powers of observation become more acute, and we can actually see our prejudices arise, noticing how we cling to fixed views. Eventually it becomes easier to relinquish them and be open to new ways of seeing. If our minds weren't fundamentally empty, we could never create a fairer society. But our naturally unbiased open mind is the source of true wisdom and compassion, and cultivating it puts us in touch with the innate value of all things.

THE PRACTICE

1. Ask a partner or friend about a bias they perceive that you have.
2. Brace yourself.
3. What is it like to hear it? Do you agree?
4. Now try it on and see if you can see it for yourself.
5. Can you relinquish it for a moment? Should you?

9   *A History of Injury*

> You cannot use cruelty against yourself to justify cruelty to others. You cannot harden your heart to the future just because of your past.
>
> —Marie Lu, *The Midnight Star*

As human beings, we share the universal experience of suffering. Each of us encounters sickness, old age, and death, and we are challenged by the demands these make on us in life. We also inherit tremendous pain through our family lineages and in our immediate family, and whether it is accidental, deliberate, or systematic, our people have either been harmed or caused great harm to others, or both, through age-old patterns of aggression, injustice, and war. In the United States we have inherited the brutal legacy of slavery, the genocide of Native peoples, and the subjugation of women in society, to name a few. We are working to correct these abuses, but the harm persists as part of our shared history, and this often forms the basis of new injuries.

In some of her work researching peace and conflict around the world, Kim found herself face-to-face with the reality of the violence that afflicts humanity and the planet every day. Looking closely into any of these conflict situations, she learned that most people long for this violence to cease and want to find ways to stop it from being repeated from generation to generation. Even while making demands for justice, most people want to find enduring ways to live fairly and peacefully.

Because we have such a long history of human injury, finding ways to process historical pain is vital to the restoration of peaceful societies. As one peace-builder friend expressed to Kim, "We need to find ways to reconcile our pain so that it does not become the seed of new resentment, new conflict, and new source of injury to others." Our history confirms the importance of this. Since 2003, every civil war that has started has been a continuation of a previous civil war.[1] This suggests that the problem has less to do with preventing new conflicts from arising and is more about finding a permanent resolution to those conflicts already present. If we are to interrupt the destructive, vengeful cycles that appear in our countries, communities, and personal relationships, we need to find more constructive ways to process our injuries and pain.

Talking about Pain

It is an important step in our emotional development to see that all human beings have pain, and to listen to how that pain is experienced differently. But it isn't easy to talk about pain, nor is it easy to hear about it. Pain is often held privately—what to share and how to share is a deeply personal choice. While there is wisdom in holding pain privately, in many contexts today we are learning to express our pain, both individually and collectively, with more care and sensitivity, and thus with a greater opportunity for healing.

We all have suffering in common, but there are real differences in the types of injuries and the severity of suffering that people have endured. We should acknowledge the distinction between suffering due to life circumstances, and suffering inflicted because of discrimination and persecution. These latter harms are inflicted precisely *because* someone is black, transgender, Muslim, or Christian, for example. These situations are ones in which people experience a threat to their existence, and for some communities, this threat has been present for generations and is the source of individual and collective trauma.

Trauma is a complex phenomenon. There are some conversations that require real sensitivity to prevent re-traumatization, the triggering of distressing psychological, emotional, and physiological consequences.[2] For example, careless, aggressive, or doubtful questions about a traumatic sexual assault can evoke feelings of powerlessness and humiliation for anyone who has suffered such an attack, compromising their potential for healing through conversation. But with enough safety and trust, an injured person can choose to open and share. And when others are simply present and listen, there is an opportunity for healing, support, and recognition of the powerful and innate resilience of people.

Navigating these conversations can feel intimidating and perilous due to the risk of causing more harm. Yet with a commitment to these difficult talks, we expand the possibility for a deeper, more holistic connection. We can ask ourselves what kinds of encounters and ways of sharing our injuries can help to reconcile our pain? What are the elements of conversation that can support a safe dialogue? How can we validate highly distinct experiences of historical pain, while at the same time forge a common bond and strengthen our mutual commitment to creating a better future?

Bearing Witness

Bearing witness is one way to transform our history of injury. This practice involves simply being present to one another when we have been hurt. It's about relating to reality as it is, not how we wish it to be. Through the process of bearing witness, we realize that historical injustice, injury, and trauma are not abstract, but are a collection of poignant lived experiences of distinct individuals.[3]

Gabriel recently led a process for people of color and white people to share and learn from one another's experience for the sake of building bridges. The topic they were exploring was their encounters with the police. In one exchange, Jason, a twenty-eight-year-old black man, shared his experience about a time when he was pulled over by the police because the registration on his license plate had expired. For him, this moment was fraught with tremendous anxiety and fear. He couldn't reassure himself that it was only a minor infraction and that he would simply be given a small fine or a warning. For Jason, this experience was connected to the larger context of slavery, racism, and police brutality that has killed unarmed black people at twice the rate of unarmed white people.[4] He couldn't imagine just getting a ticket; instead, he imagined being shot.

Once he pulled over to the side of the road, he saw a black officer step out of the police car. He relaxed, immediately relieved by the fact that he and the officer shared a racial identity. As he composed himself, he leaned over to open his glove compartment to retrieve his registration, only to have his anxiety shoot up again when he caught sight of another police officer, a white man, with his hand on his holster, approaching from the other side of the car. Jason felt overwhelming anxiety and at the same time immense pressure to remain calm. He was fearful the police might overreact, so in an effort to steady himself he started to pray. And as he prayed he felt all of his accomplishments draining away: graduating from a prestigious university, being the captain of a Division I varsity team, becoming a successful entrepreneur working to make a positive impact, and participating in his deep Christian faith. None of these things mattered in this moment. He was sure that the officers simply saw a black man, one who was possibly unpredictable and threatening. All he had, he said, was his prayer.

As he spoke to the other participants in the workshop, Jason relived the experience. The vulnerability and terror he felt with those police officers showed through his wide-open eyes and firm yet vulnerable words. When he finished, a potent silence remained, but a woman spoke up, energized and anxious. "What happened to you is awful! I am part of a group of activists that is combating white supremacy and police brutality."

Gabriel gently said to the woman, "I appreciate the work you're doing, but in this moment let's simply be present for Jason and what he shared." Later, Gabriel reflected with the group on the interaction between Jason and the woman. He said, "Often, other people's distress causes us distress, so it's natural that we want to relieve someone of a difficult memory or emotional experience. But when we act from a place of anxiety, trying to fix or alleviate the pain, we inadvertently shift the attention to ourselves, and we may miss the opportunity to affirm someone else's truth, to bear witness to them, and to further understand the inside of their experience."

Learning to bear witness also means being present to yourself, including your impulse to want to remedy or change someone else's experience. But in simply being present, a quiet and attentive witness, deeply listening, you can internalize what it was like to be the other person in that situation, like Jason, when he felt that all he had was his prayer.

How Should We Listen?

Peace circles are a type of talking circle, which are part of cultural traditions all over the world, including Native peoples of North America, Nigeria, Kenya, and Uganda.[5] Circles provide a safe structure for people to express sensitive matters, with the intention of creating mutual understanding and connection.

A few years ago, Kim participated in a peacemaking circle training in New York with Kay Pranis. A soft-spoken leader in the field of restorative justice, Kay has developed the use of peace circles to facilitate listening, understanding, and responding to historical harms done to groups of people; in turn, this supports efforts to address racial, economic, and gender inequities that persist today.[6]

On the first day of the weekend-long training, most of the twenty-five attendees were strangers to one another, remaining somewhat aloof and professional in their tone. The second day opened with a round of check-ins to share any overnight reflections, which is common for this kind of group work. The participants took turns, patiently moving around the circle from person to person, passing the "talking piece." Kay had chosen a small hunk of worn, pale driftwood that sat snugly and satisfyingly in each hand, naturally inviting introspection.

After about a third of the people in the circle had spoken, the group gently turned their attention to the next woman in the circle. She began to share memories about a parent with whom she had suffered a long-term abusive relationship. As she spoke, she connected deeply with herself and with her feelings of vulnerability, grief, regret, and helplessness in that relationship. At some point she looked around and saw the rest of the people in the circle listening intently, simply holding space for her without pity, judgment, or the need to comfort her. She paused, receiving that unconditional attention. When she was finished, she wiped away her tears, breathed deeply a few times, and passed the talking piece to the next person.

Kim felt a palpable shift in the entire feeling of the room, which had been catalyzed by the woman's honest expression and the willingness of others to listen. Following her contribution, others volunteered personal stories about injuries and harms they had suffered, including recollections of physical attacks, abuse, or abandonment. What prompted others to share? Whether it was to create solidarity in the group, to process injuries together, or to relieve the loneliness of their own stories, they offered their intimate narratives without defensiveness or anxiety. The circle had become a humble container of listening, and a powerful one. By the end of the training, Kim no longer felt professional distance, but instead felt the closeness of everyone in the group. At the close of the day, everyone voiced sincere gratitude for their time together, sounding almost wistful for more connection as they said their goodbyes.

Kim left the experience pondering how this impromptu healing circle had organically emerged, and why the opportunity to disclose highly personal and tender parts of themselves was taken up by so many. The safe environment, quality of listening, and one person's willingness to express openly and vulnerably had catalyzed others to follow in kind, providing a natural invitation for people to speak up.

The group's unconditional presence seemed to soften the compulsive need to offer solutions or remedies. There was permission to simply reflect on the past without pressure to "get over it." In other words, people were allowed to speak, to remember, and to feel, while the others simply listened and witnessed, without blame or judgment. In the words of the famous Gestalt psychologist Fritz Perls, "Awareness per se of and by itself can be curative."[7] Being held in others' attention in the circle uncondi-tionally supported healing.

Painting the Cracks with Gold

Last summer, Kim's friend had a favorite black mug smashed to pieces by his cat, who enjoys pushing things off the table. Noticing her friend's crestfallen face as they picked up the pieces together, she told him about the traditional Japanese art of *kintsugi*, where broken pottery is mended with gold resin or lacquer so that the cracks are illuminated rather than concealed. With a sense of duty and love, they carefully glued the shards back together and traced the cracks with thin lines of shimmering gold paint. As if to symbolize scars from life experiences, the striking gold lines highlighted the imperfections and kept the event of change mean-ingful and alive. This ancient process embodies the Japanese philosophy of *mushin*, or no mind/heart, wherein the concepts of nonattachment and acceptance of change are considered integral aspects of human life and existence.

The way that we remember our own life-shattering events is impor-tant. There is immense power in retelling and integrating such events. There is a danger, of course, that we become so identified with our pain that we create more suffering for ourselves. While it is important to ac-knowledge the ways in which we may have been traumatized, it is also important not to assume the identity of a victim. A Tibetan Buddhist teacher says, "If an arrow wounds you, you can blame the one who shot the arrow for your injury. But if you then take that arrow and grind it deeper and deeper into your wound, that is your own doing."[8]

Practicing nonattachment to suffering means that we accept our pain, and we also see that we are far more than it. When pain is acknowledged, it can be released. There is freedom in finding distance not only from our injuries but also from all of our experiences, memories, and preoccupa-tion with ourselves. In Zen we cultivate this recognition of what is known as *emptiness*, the freedom from our stories, identity, and self-referencing.

Because we are fundamentally empty, that is, capable of letting go, we have the capacity for healing and forgiveness.

Like the practice of mending broken pots with gold resin, we can be inspired to find meaningful and sacred ways of talking about and receiving one another's recollections of injury. And yet, as we attend to the cracks lovingly, we cannot forget about the body of the pot itself and the motivations behind the act of mending. Our life is based on the principle that whatever hurts other people hurts us; that the injustices experienced by others are also injustices experienced by us. None of us can truly be free, fulfilled, and empowered unless we are working to ensure that everyone can be free, fulfilled, and empowered.

We value a sincere kind of wholeness in our relationships and our experiences. When we return our attention to the whole, we see the whole pot: its shape and size, its form and function, the golden cracks and the still-formed panels. It has the greatest potential when it is empty. By communing with our shared history of suffering, we can appreciate our imperfect yet precious humanity. And from that point of deep connection, we elevate our chances for a happier shared future.

THE PRACTICE

1. Take time to reflect on an injury in your life.
2. Is there a story that you tell others about what happened?
3. Think about the people you have told the story to and how they were able to be present to deeply listen to you.
4. Set the intention to be present and listen, without fixing, judging, or trying to comfort the speaker the next time someone shares a story of injury with you.

10   *Strong Emotions in Conversation*

Feel, he told himself, feel, feel, feel. Even if what you feel is
pain, only let yourself feel.

—P. D. James, *The Children of Men*

This is a strange and painful story.

A friend of ours, Jon, is Jewish and was raised in upstate New York. He
is retired now and spends his summers with his wife in a small western
town, enjoying the open spaces and beauty. One summer he went to visit
the local dentist. He was sitting comfortably in the dentist's chair. The
dentist had already done the procedure, and they were waiting for the ce-
ment to set. While they were waiting, Jon and the dentist began making
small talk. In a short time, the conversation led to the dentist's father and
his role as a US undercover agent in Berlin during World War II. Soon,
the dentist walked out of the room and returned with something to show
Jon. His father had brought back a dagger used by Hitler's youth corps. It
was inscribed with a swastika and the German words for "blood and soil."

Can you imagine what it was like to be Jon in this moment? Like so
many Jews his age, he grew up immersed in the legacy of the Holocaust,
including the loss of many of his extended family. He described sitting

in this chair, his mouth immobilized, unable to speak very well, experiencing a wave of fear-filled memories. He was entirely unclear about the dentist's motive in showing him this object. The dentist knew he was Jewish but probably never had much contact with Jewish people before. At a certain point he simply told the dentist very straightforwardly that he felt extremely vulnerable. The dentist seemed to immediately register Jon's feelings and quickly slipped out of the room, taking the knife with him.

Telling this story in vivid detail, Jon shared a wide range of feeling states, from quizzical and confused, to scared, vulnerable, and finally, relieved. The most poignant moment in his story came when he recounted simply stating his vulnerability to the dentist. He didn't attribute malice or ill will to him, surprisingly so, nor did he blame him for his predicament. He concluded that the dentist's behavior was due to his ignorance and was an inept attempt to share something they appeared to have in common.

Hearing this story was painful and disturbing, and reading about it here probably is as well. Conversations related to our differences often produce strong feeling states, including fear. Anger over injustice, sorrow due to loss, fear of making mistakes, or guilt over the past often accompany and embellish our conversations. When these emotions arise, they are powerful and pertinent. They infuse the atmosphere with meaning and depth, but they can also convey threat and uncertainty. Strong emotions bring people together, but just as often they set people apart. For anyone who wants to engage in wholehearted discussions, it is essential to develop the capacity to be present to strong feeling states in yourself and in others. What makes Jon's story notable is his willingness to simply name his feelings, and this gesture quickly changed the dynamics of the situation.

The Spectrum of Feelings

Emotions are an essential part of the human experience, but how we relate to them varies significantly. Since the release of Daniel Goleman's seminal book *Emotional Intelligence*,[1] there is growing recognition that we can develop the capacity to be aware of and express our emotions. Emotions are extremely intelligent, informative, and energetic, but working with them is an art, one that requires intention. The problem is that there are very few contexts that support looking deeply into emotional states and little instruction for learning how to feel them fully and how to release them completely. Most of this learning takes place in therapeutic contexts, although today some embodiment coaches, teachers, and spiritual guides are equipped to provide direction.

Conversation is a place where people can practice working with emotional states because they elicit so much feeling. We work to support people in acknowledging and including their emotions so that our conversations are deep, nuanced, and enriched with feeling. Feelings bring people to life; they communicate powerfully and immediately. Unlike language, feelings convey meaning directly, bringing coherence to groups because there are no boundaries when it comes to people's emotions.[2] While the positive emotions of others are generally easy to experience and join with, it's more difficult to be present to negative or painful emotions. These more challenging emotions can derail conversations, shut down participation, or provoke resentment or withdrawal. So they have to be worked with very carefully.

In learning about emotions, it is helpful to begin by making several distinctions. First, we need to practice locating the corresponding sensations in the body—for example, trembling in the hands, constriction in the throat, or pressure in the head. These sensations can be intense, chaotic, or overwhelming. Sometimes we have to practice noting sensations directly, without any mental interpretations, because we have such an entrenched habit of avoiding them, including medicating or dousing our sensations with food or drink. Sensations in the body become feelings when they are given names such as "fear," "sadness," or "anger." In other words, when we feel them, we quickly interpret them mentally and then assign a label to them.

Full-blown emotions arise when the feedback loop between our thoughts and the embodied sensations is synced-up and running.[3] For example, we might experience the direct sensations of anger as pressure in the head, clenching in the jaws, higher volume in the voice, heat in the face, and gripping in the arms and hands. At the same time, our mind is likely filled with thoughts and judgments like "I'm so pissed," "He was unfair," or "I'm going to put a stop to that!" The more we generate thoughts associated with the feeling state, the more the feelings are amplified and sustained. Sensations give rise to thoughts and labels, and thoughts and labels reinforce sensations in an ongoing feedback loop. That is why some emotions can last for days. When this cycle between thoughts and feelings occurs frequently, forming a habitual emotional pattern, it deepens into a characteristic of our personality, as in "a happy person," "a hothead," or "a nervous wreck."

There are times in conversation when slowing down and simply *feeling* for a moment can be extremely helpful. It is sometimes relieving to pause and turn our attention directly to the body, noticing just the physical sensations. We can ask ourselves, *Where are the sensations located? What is their texture or qualities? How they are moving or changing?* Once sensation is experienced directly, we can ask for the name of the feeling, eliciting words like *fear, anger,* or *sadness.* This labeling helps us connect even more deeply with our embodied experience, rather than simply coping with it. Next, we can look for what thoughts come up in relation to the sensations. By learning to pay close attention, we can interrupt the habitual mind-body feedback loop,[4] and we become much more aware, fresh, and considered in what we want to say.

Fear

Fear is one of our most basic emotions. It is caused by a perceived threat or danger and is felt as increased heart rate, sweaty palms, dry mouth, nausea, restlessness in the limbs, and an impulse to move or get away. These symptoms are caused by the stimulation of the fight-or-flight response and an increase in the production of stress hormones in the body.[5] Anxiety, a form of fear, arises in anticipation of a threat, but often the threat may be nonspecific, unknown, or uncontrollable, whereas fear is usually in response to a very here-and-now sense of danger.

Fear is essentially the pure recognition that we are alive and subject to being hurt and dying. Fear can be viewed as the emotion that connects us to the intrinsic fact of our life, to its value and the deep, unwavering instinct to preserve it. As Jon's story demonstrates, fear reveals our vulnerability and often our tenderness.

When there is fear present in conversation and it is unacknowledged, it has a stifling effect. People will stammer, and their speech will become halting. Speakers appear to be second-guessing themselves, and the flow of energy stops. There is stress in the conversation, and strain. Sometimes people will try to please listeners with their words in an unconscious attempt to relieve the fear, but because their messages are ambiguous or uncertain, listeners don't do a good job in hearing them. They become impatient or irritable because they are sensing fear in their own bodies. These are all signs pointing to unacknowledged fear in the conversation. It is best to try to locate the fear in yourself and name it, or help others do the same. When you do this, if you follow Jon's example and share your feelings, you'll be surprised how relieving it is.

Anger

Anger can be extremely energizing in conversation, but it's also dangerous because it quickly becomes destructive to relationships. However, anger's destructive nature is its power. Sometimes patterns or structures need to be destroyed in order for evolution to take place. Sometimes we have to get fed up with the status quo in order to make necessary changes, like leaving a toxic relationship, quitting a job, or challenging an unjust system. There is a push in the anger; it runs hot in the body and makes a demand on us and others. Anger is immediate, urgent, and like a lightning storm, it booms with light and truth.

When we clarify anger, taking responsibility for ourselves and our truth, it reveals our deep caring—what we stand for, what we will fight for, and what our limits and boundaries are. It increases the life force in the body, and it also has a great impact in the room when used skillfully.

It carries with it a sense of personal power and conviction, and it can have tremendous positive influence on others. In short, righteous anger can be very enlivening to a system.

On the other hand, anger and the push that accompanies it almost always stimulates some level of fear when it is directed at other people. In the context of our facilitated conversations, we sometimes have to help soothe people when they get excessively angry. Otherwise it becomes very difficult for others to receive their message because the flight-or-fight response is intense. Sometimes people reject that idea, however, asserting that we should be able to tolerate the expression of self-righteous anger, particularly in the context of discussions about injustice.

That's true when anger is held in the first-person "I" perspective and owned, but when it is directed intensely at others, at "you," the fight-or-flight response will take over, and although others appear to be listening, they're simply coping. The calm that is necessary in the body in order for people to think and listen clearly is disrupted in the presence of even mild threat. This is not a strength or character issue; it's the result of evolutionary biology. So there's a place for righteous anger, and there are also limits to its usefulness.

One of the biggest challenges with anger is knowing when to let go of it. We can be loyal to our principles without becoming stuck in our anger. We want to be available to anger's energy and its intelligence, but we don't want it to become a defining characteristic of our personality, so when we run hot we may want to work at containing it. But when there is a tendency to contain anger, it might help to learn to express it more directly. Err on the side of making "I" statements when expressing anger and avoid projecting it onto "you." If you turn the focus onto others, your communication will inevitably lose its power to persuade.

Sadness

Robert Augustus Masters, a relationship expert, Integral psychotherapist, and psychospiritual guide and trainer, has written a very good book titled

Emotional Intimacy. He refers to sadness as "loss taken to heart." [6] Sadness is a poignant and sensitive response to life's disappointments and losses. The experience of sorrow can be debilitating in a way that anger and fear are not. When sadness comes over us, we want to turn inward, retreat, collapse, or curl into a fetal position to simply attend to the feelings.

When sadness comes into a conversation, it registers immediately. It's as if hearts are wired together, and as one person dips into sorrow, most everyone else does simultaneously. But unlike fear, which can go unnoticed, or anger, which commands attention, sadness seems to be an emotion that people experience but usually want to dispel quickly, especially in the company of others, to preserve one's social presentation.

When sadness is felt or expressed, others will frequently try to comfort, either to soothe the distress in themselves or in the person expressing the sadness. So when sadness does occur in conversation, it's important to create space for it. This can happen by allowing some silence for a moment just to feel, or by naming the sadness and legitimizing it. When sadness is accommodated in this way, inevitably it helps to make us more tender, real human beings, keeping us in touch with our compassion, our care, and our goodwill toward others.

Grief is a full-blown, acute emotional process, usually due to a significant loss. Within grief there is the intense feeling of sorrow and heartbreak; there could be a loss of appetite, intense distractedness, and a sensation of a deep hole in the center of the body. There can be a watery, wavelike quality to grief, and there may be lots of tears, which is one of the reasons why we are so defended against this feeling. We fear it will overwhelm us and that we will drown in it. In time, we learn to surrender to the waves and allow ourselves to really cry. If we release fully into crying, we may find that we are lighter, more tender, and softer because of it.

Sometimes grief will show up in conversation, and depending on the context, allowing room for the expression of grief can be helpful. People will often become silent and sit quietly together for a few minutes. It could be appropriate to ask the person, "Would you like to talk about what you're feeling?" and assure them that crying is perfectly appropriate to the conversation. However, if someone is really grieving, we may need to pause and find a way to give them extra emotional support outside of the context of conversation. In this way it is important to make a distinction between the ordinary experience of sadness and the upwelling of grief. And it's always helpful to recommend getting the support of grief counseling, if the person hasn't already.

White Fragility

Robin DiAngelo, an antiracism educator, has written about a phenomenon she calls "white fragility."[7] She describes a common experience of white people who, when trying to enter into a dialogue about racism, find the stress of the discussion intolerable, and this triggers "a range of defensive moves. These moves include the outward display of emotions such as anger, fear, and guilt, and behaviors such as argumentation, silence, and leaving the stress-inducing situation. These behaviors, in turn, function to reinstate white racial equilibrium."[8] In other words, when those of us who are white fail to remain present, to listen and learn from the experience of people of color, we literally participate in keeping the status quo intact. If we can't participate fully on the level of conversation, how do we expect to meaningfully participate in relationship building, social change initiatives, and sustained advocacy?

In our context, we usually see this fragility arise when people are new to conversations about race. If participants don't have a lot of experience working with their emotional states, feelings of guilt, anger, sadness, and other strong feelings can overwhelm their attention. This kind of fragility can be an obstruction to talking straight and to listening well, and as DiAngelo asserts, it can interfere with efforts to create real change.

When this form of defensiveness arises, whether in a personal conversation or a group discussion, remember that there's nothing wrong with experiencing strong emotions, as long as the emotions don't obstruct the conversation. Try to give yourself and others an opportunity to feel fully, and then to practice listening and reflecting on what you've heard. As people gain more experience in this, their tolerance for their strong feelings increases and their ability to stay present in the conversation thus improves. Over time, they develop stamina and can model for others how to stay engaged, even when the conversation is challenging to the nervous system. When everyone can engage with more emotional stability, more effective conversations can occur.

Emotional Maturity

Cultivating emotional maturity takes intention and sustained effort. It is extremely helpful to have a therapist, coach, or guide when learning to navigate our own interiors.

When we begin to work with our feelings, we usually inhabit one of two polarities: we either dwell or drown in emotions, or we attempt to bypass feelings entirely. We all have the capacity to feel and emote, as well as to ignore or disregard feelings. But depending on our culture and family history, we may be one-sided in our relationship to our emotions.

As we develop, we learn to balance between feeling and letting go, rather than one or the other. Little children are good examples of how emotions can come and go quickly. They emote fully, and they recalibrate easily when comforted because they are not yet anchored to cognitive narratives that keep emotions alive. Developing emotional maturity means that we have learned to experience the sensations and feelings directly, allowing them to blossom and inform, and release them without a trace. The challenge for adults is to let go of the thoughts that energize the emotions when they are no longer useful.

The application of mindfulness, paying close attention to activity in our nervous system, can help us grow in emotional maturity. The following is a seven-step process that can help us learn to experience sensations immediately, name the feelings, and become familiar with the feedback loop between sensations and thoughts. We can actively practice interrupting this feedback loop while at the same time learn to receive the intelligence and energy of the emotions.

Transmuting Emotions: A Process

I. Feel bodily sensations. The first step is to feel the physical sensations in your body. Notice particular areas like your stomach, solar plexus, heart, throat, or jaw. Allow yourself to feel sensations like swirling, gripping, aching, vibrating, and how these sensations move and change. Remember not to judge anything as being good or bad, right or wrong, but do note whether the feelings are pleasant or unpleasant. If they are either too chaotic or overwhelming, focus on your inhalation and exhalation to help manage the experience.

2. Name the feeling. The second step is to engage your cognition. Feel the sensations, and then name those feelings. There are lists of the names of emotions on the web.[9] Having a greater vocabulary to describe one's emotions can actually help you discern more subtlety in your feeling states; in fact, studies have shown that even the simple act of naming negative emotions can help you dispel their unruly nature.[10] This is the beginning of witnessing how the body and mind interact to create emotions.

3. Watch the mind-body feedback loop. Notice how thoughts reinforce the sensations in your body, and how sensations stimulate thoughts. This feedback loop is what gives rise to a full-blown emotion.

4. Drop the story. This means hitting "pause" on thoughts and storylines. This step is necessary to interrupt the feedback loop, but it's not as easy as it sounds. Mental activity literally helps us escape the discomfort in the body, so it takes quite a bit of mindfulness to put the mind on hold and bring your attention back to your body. By stepping out of the narrative, however, your mind relaxes and your body can begin to recalibrate.

5. Experience the energy and intelligence of the emotion. Now that your mind is quiet and you have begun to recalibrate your body, just feel the energy of the feeling directly. Notice the aliveness of the emotion. When you feel

ready, you can ask: *What's right about this feeling or emotion?* Notice that the thoughts you have now are, most likely, more alive and current than the habitual story you may have been telling yourself earlier.

6. Let go. Allow the emotions, feelings, and sensations to subside. Sometimes, because letting go is so difficult, "letting be" may be necessary before "letting go" is possible.

7. Decide whether to communicate your feelings. Emotions are a powerful, connecting, and sensitizing force in our communications, and expressing them can create intimacy, strengthening our bonds with others, and providing greater nuance and depth to our relationships.

Communicating Feelings

One of the important questions to consider when working with emotions is how, and whether, to communicate what we are feeling. When do we choose to share our feelings in conversation, and why?

There are many environments, such as corporate settings or other businesses, where the focus on productivity excludes emotions because they are perceived as irrational and inefficient. While emotions are not rational processes, they are a tremendous source of information, and they can be expressed extremely efficiently. In fact, it's only when people haven't learned how to express emotions clearly that they are inefficient at work. The act of expressing emotions doesn't have to be overly dramatic or dreadful, nor does it have to involve hours of processing. It's possible to touch on the emotion, name it, receive its message, and then move on.

Emotional maturity also means taking responsibility for our feeling states rather than projecting them onto others. This is a continual learning process as we gain deeper insight into our habitual patterns and the emotions we tend to experience, and the ways in which we make others responsible for them. The more we own our own feeling states, the freer we are of them.

Appreciating Positive Feeling States

As we learn to work with emotions typically considered negative, more space is created for recognizing positive emotions. People generally notice negative emotions more often than positive ones. Rick Hanson, a writer on the neuroscience of happiness,[11] says, "The brain is like Velcro for negative experiences but Teflon for positive experiences." He notes that one negative interaction in an important relationship is five times more powerful than a positive interaction.[12] Most of us have a negativity bias, that is, we tend to forget positive emotions while retaining the memory of negative ones. This, of course, stems from the evolutionary predisposition to learn from the mistakes and errors that create pain or suffering. If we have a habit of ignoring our feelings, we may also be diminished in our ability to experience positive states like joy, bliss, or happiness.

Part of the practice of including positive emotions is, as with negative emotions, learning to expand our vocabulary and be able to name more of the subtler shades or flavors of these positive feeling states. It may be easy to use words like *joy* and *bliss*, but it's valuable to seek out words like *ebullient*, *effervescent*, *upbeat*, and *ecstatic* in order to expand our range and capacity to recognize more gradations of the emotions.

Practicing recognition of our positive feeling states supports our conversations and our relationships. We can develop a habit of noticing what went well and how good it felt to speak openly or be listened to. We can employ the ground rule of using praise to actively pay attention to positive experiences and feeling states. Thinking back to the conversation with Jon about his story at the dentist's office, it would be easy to remember what went wrong that day. Instead, remembering Jon's authenticity, his willingness to be responsible for his emotions, and his forgiveness of the dentist leave a positive imprint on the mind and heart.

THE PRACTICE

Practice the seven-step process on emotional transmutation. Remember that the first three steps are related to letting the emotion be, without repressing or changing it. Then we suspend the narrative and with the help of the breath, begin self-regulation. As the body begins to calm down, we can then ask, *What is right about this feeling?* This should result in a fresh perspective on the emotional response.

11   *Clarifying Power*

Nearly all men can stand adversity, but if you want to test a man's character, give him power.

—Unknown

Burning Man is an annual event where for one week a city is temporarily erected out in the middle of the Nevada desert. It's a Bay Area version of a Dionysian festival, full of artists, explorers, innovators, psychonauts, and people who straight-up like to party. Burning Man is known for the very strong and reliable container it creates for the over sixty thousand people who attend the event. It has been described as an experiment in art and community, held together by ten shared principles, including self-responsibility, a gift economy, and leave no trace. It utilizes sophisticated urban design and civic structures and offers its own mental health services, communications support, and emergency medical team. The purpose of the event is to invite people to explore new and creative ways of being oneself and being with others. In honor of that, it culminates in a powerful ritual of burning "The Man," a giant wooden effigy and its support structure, which is like watching a three-story building go up in flames out in the middle of nowhere.

Diane went to Burning Man with several friends, one of whom is a leader of an organization that had begun to experiment with a flat, horizontal organizational structure and consensus decision-making. He was deeply interested in applying participatory leadership to all aspects of his organization in order to distribute power more evenly. He was so excited about this new approach that he wouldn't stop talking about it, bordering on some serious zealotry. So Diane said to him, "I agree that there are contexts and situations when flatter, more distributed governance structures can enhance how we collaborate and work together. But verticality also has its benefits, especially when it comes to efficiency, clarity, and maintaining energy with a strong sense of direction." Her friend flatly disagreed. Hierarchies of all kinds were out, as far as he was concerned.

Later that night, Diane and her friend went out to the playa to explore different sound camps, pop-up music clubs where DJs spin electronic dance music against a dark, starry sky punctuated by LEDs and strobe lights. People put in all-nighters, dancing in one club and then the next, while the DJ is elevated four stories above the crowd, laying down beats like an Olympian god. Diane's friend was completely enthralled by one particular DJ and the whole scene. Diane smiled, gave him a jab with her elbow, and said, "I notice you're enjoying the hierarchy now."

An electronic dance party is probably not the best example of the different ways power can be distributed, used, or abused, but it does illustrate the point. Power is an integral aspect of the human experience. It permeates all our relationships and informs our projects and endeavors. While it may be structured vertically, horizontally, or a combination of both, it is always at play. It can be worked with consciously, with an intention to benefit everyone, or selectively, to benefit just a few. It can be wielded carefully, judiciously, with consent and restraint, or it can be completely abused. But since power is energy, it cannot be destroyed.

What Is Power?

First of all, what is power? Power, in our conversations, refers to the ability to galvanize energy, influence others, and mobilize resources to achieve desired goals. An Integral model would locate power arising in four different dimensions: [1]

1. A person's deep, internal strengths, like intelligence, creativity, spiritual depth, or moral authority, are a signature of power.
2. A person's external behaviors and observable traits, like physical strength, athleticism, or beauty, are dimensions of power. Talent is a major form of power, as is business acumen. Put those two together and you have the makings of star power.
3. Cultural contexts afford influence and access to resources, a dimension of power. For example, society affords status to people based on skin color, gender, or financial means. It also confers positions such as an elected leader, an executive in a company, or in the case of a first lady, being the spouse of a US president. Power may extend from a role such as newspaper editor, columnist, author, or musician, but all of these require a profound cultural context as well.
4. External structures promote the distribution of power via systems, structures, institutions, or natural resources. Furthermore, to have significant social power, a uniquely persuasive individual voice must be combined with a highly organized and well-financed delivery system, such as a publishing or record company, to reach a large audience, or these days a large following on social media.

There are highly complicated forms of power that combine all four of these dimensions. Political prowess, military might, and economic strength are made up of a complex and dynamic combination of lots of people, talent, roles, money, resources, values, and organized structures and systems. To accrue and maintain power, these complex systems must have excellent timing, durability, and a capacity to execute successfully again and again. Once these structures and systems are put into place, however, they can serve to keep certain groups of people in power positions while locking other groups out through lack of opportunity, education, access, and other forms of discrimination.

Power Abuse

Where there is power, there is the potential for misuse or abuse. It can be a person who abuses it, such as an angry parent, a manipulative lover, a dominating boss, or a corrupt politician. Cultures maintain strongly held belief systems of superiority and inferiority and then work hard to enact those beliefs. Systems are also abusive. Banking systems can exploit their clients with hidden fees and inflated interest rates. Police can harass citizens, misusing their authority to make stops and arrests, and shooting unarmed people. Corporations can take advantage of employees by overworking and underpaying them, and exploit all their stakeholders by only looking out for the interests of their shareholders. Churches can abuse; so can governments, and they do, often with impunity. Again, where there is power, there can be abuse. It is our evolutionary challenge to become more conscious of the use of power so that it serves the good of all, and find strategies for preventing its abuse. That's why conversations about power are so prevalent today.

Conversations related to social justice, for the most part, focus on power dynamics: examining the unfair distribution of power and resources, identifying how complex systems serve to keep some groups on top, and exploring ways to change these patterns. There is an attempt to right past wrongs and address the resulting inequities that are still occurring today. The emergence of words like *decolonization, patriarchy, white supremacy*, and so on are words that identify the power structures that have, and do, privilege certain groups at the expense of others.

Power in Conversation

In conversations about power in the context of human relations, there is always the recognition of those who have power vis-à-vis those who don't. Having power implies not having it; having more power points to having less. This isn't the case when we talk about the power of rocket fuel or solar power—those refer to pure sources of energy. But in human conversation, the perception of one-up/one-down dynamics regarding power is almost always at play. Our job is not only to help people talk *about* power but, more importantly, to help people see how different forms of power are being used, and sometimes misused, in conversation.

Randee Levine, a good friend of Diane's, is a longtime student of Arnold Mindell, a Jungian analyst, teacher, and author. Their Processwork learning community has examined the phenomenon of power in relationship for decades.[2] Diane has learned a lot from Randee, particularly about the specific ways to spot one-up/one-down dynamics in conversation. Randee says that when we are in the position of being one-up, we are confident and comfortable in ourselves and our perspective. We might even feel smug, like we are on the inside and understand the rules of the game. We feel free to sit back, relax, and contribute, or not. When we do speak first, we will often set the tone for engagement. Usually we are less emotional when we are on top, more able to be rational, chill, and less easily offended. Often, however, we may fail to see the problem at hand; in fact, we may not even acknowledge the perspectives of others, but instead stick to our own viewpoint. We may judge others for being overly reactive or too sensitive and feel that it is our job to help everyone get on with the agenda.

The reverse is true when we find ourselves one-down. We may feel anxious, uncertain, or like we don't belong. We may find it difficult to speak or express ourselves and will sometimes rehearse what we want to say before we say it. We often feel more emotional, angry, teary, or upset. There is an inability to be clear. Sometimes we attempt to please or placate the others, but these attempts are usually unsuccessful. We may have more bodily signs of anxiety, like shaking, sweating, or looking away. Overall, we may feel hopeless or misunderstood. And, needless to say, whoever is in the one-down position feels less effective, competent, and available.

Gabe facilitated a conversation between men and women who work together at a technology company in the Bay Area. The women were voicing their challenges, concerns, and frustrations with how frequently they felt one-down, unseen, or disempowered. As the men listened, Gabe asked them to reflect what they had heard the women say. This was to ensure that the men understood, and that the women actually felt heard. Gabe invited some of the men to share how they were impacted by what they heard.

Thomas raised his hand and said, "I'm very touched by what you said, and I'm sorry about all the negative experiences you've had with me and with us." He paused, feeling carefully into what he wanted to say next. "I want to simply express that all the pre-work, and especially what you shared today, have really opened my eyes. I'm learning so much. I want you to know that you have an ally in me."

Rachel quickly said, "What have you learned?" Gabe felt his anxiety shoot up. Her tone was skeptical, challenging even, although Thomas had seemed sincere in attempting to create an alliance with her and the women in the room. A few minutes earlier, when the women had been speaking, they had seemed to be in a one-down position, but now their energy was one-up. The power dynamic, at least in this moment, appeared to have shifted right in front of Gabe's eyes.

Thomas replied, likely feeling some anxiety himself because at this point his words were more jumbled than before. He seemed to struggle to respond. He tried producing a coherent insight or two, but he appeared not to be very clear about what he had just learned. As soon as he paused, Rachel followed up with, "What else have you learned?"

Gabe intervened, posing a question to Rachel and Thomas: "Can we slow down for a moment? I'm curious about how you are both feeling right now."

"I'm feeling fine," said Rachel.

"Can you give me some more details?" inquired Gabe.

"I feel calm, but also energized. My mind is clear, and I feel confident in what I have to say," she said.

Gabe thanked her, and invited Thomas to speak.

"I feel anxious, a little foggy, with an impulse to withdraw and protect myself. I notice I want to measure up, but I can't. I know Rachel wants to hear something from me, but I feel like I'm coming off as inadequate or something."

Gabe reflected back what he had heard each of them say and pointed out that their descriptions fit the felt experience of a one-up/one-down dynamic. Rachel was confident and relaxed in the moment. She was sure of herself, and perhaps even intimidating to Thomas. He felt disempowered, unable to contribute positively to the situation or the relationship. Nothing he tried worked. Gabe asked the group to pay special attention, because what Thomas described feeling in this moment was exactly what the women had been talking about just a few minutes earlier when they reported feeling one-down, unseen, and disempowered in the organization.

Gabe continued, "We want to try to recognize when unconscious power dynamics are at play because when they are, we are neither as effective nor as happy as we can be. So we need to practice the skills of listening, giving and receiving feedback when necessary, and creating a culture that looks at its own relationship to power. It's possible to create power *with* one another, rather than power *over* another.[3] By recognizing one-up/one-down dynamics, we can relieve them and create mutual empowerment while working together—unless, of course, you have personal aspirations to simply be a mini-dictator, and I'm fine with that as long as you own it!" People chuckled at the dictator joke, but the point was made.

Sometimes, people holding power may not always be aware of how they impact or dominate others. Kim recalls a meeting from a few years ago where that exact thing happened. She was involved in coordinating some activist efforts regarding the Palestinian-Israeli conflict. In an informal planning meeting, the conversation took a turn and led to a woman speaking up and telling her personal story at great length, in an attempt to advocate for her positions. She recounted how, as a Palestinian living in the United Kingdom, she felt desperately unsupported. Her account was vivid, with raw emotional impact. She spoke for almost an hour, while everyone else listened.

Her stories of personal oppression and discrimination were real; so was her pain. The group was very interested in hearing her speak. But as time went on, she began to lose people's attention. She minimized the work being done by students who had been organizing political actions and protests on behalf of the Palestinians for months. At one point she demonstrated the signals of being one-up by impatiently blowing off a question she was asked by a group member. At that point, people started to cast sideways glances at one another, stirring in their seats, growing more and more uncomfortable with how she was using her time. It's challenging when someone fails to notice when they are losing their audience. It may have been more supportive to her and the entire group if at some point someone would have genuinely thanked her and brought the group's attention back to its purpose.

The Conscious Use of Power

What does it mean to use power consciously? Julie Diamond, another student of Arnold Mindell, has written a very valuable book called *Power: A User's Guide*, in which she explores the path of a conscious relationship to power. If we endeavor to do this—and it is a serious undertaking—we must first be willing to acknowledge the presence of power dynamics in our relationships. Then we should study them.

The cultivation of self-awareness is key to our efforts because we all experience having power, even in the smallest ways, and we all know what it's like to have less power, to lose power, or to feel powerless. But many times we fail to notice both sides of our experience, so it is useful to learn to pay attention, noticing the signals of both poles of the one-up/one-down dynamic. We can practice occupying either end of the polarity, becoming flexible and fluid. And by listening and validating all perspectives, we can soften the power differences, exchanging in a free and flexible way, at least during conversation.

The conscious use of power always includes sharing it, distributing it, or finding new and different ways to structure it. A leader who is conscious of their power is always aware that someone else may have a better answer, vision, or insight. He or she is highly sensitive to the fact that their power is given to them by their supporters and can be taken away. People who are aware of their power and privilege will make great efforts to ensure they are empowering other voices by listening or giving the spotlight to others so they can speak or act.

Everybody should have the experience of being a dictator for a day, just to learn what it's like to be given power and then have to use it. We might start out with our head in the clouds like our DJ at Burning Man, but we will be knocked back to earth soon enough when the responsibility that comes with power becomes known. We should be awake to the potential for becoming intoxicated with power but realize how quickly that feel-good experience can lead down a slippery slope. In other words, we need to study the potential pitfalls of having power and the limitations of our own perspective, and invite feedback regularly to illuminate our blind spots. Conscious leaders will solicit feedback frequently instead of waiting for it to come to them.

The truth is, from an evolutionary biology point of view, power is a deep and abiding aspect of the human experience.[4] It is part of our growth trajectory to learn how to work with power in our relationships. We can't get rid of it, we can't disown it, and we can't neutralize it. But we can become more conscious of it, finding new ways to distribute our power, to structure it, and when we do utilize hierarchy, we can appreciate our good and steady reason for it. Above all, we can and should clarify our determination to use our power and privilege for the good of the whole.

Maybe the most important thing we should remember is that all power is transient. A judge has power in the courtroom, but comes home to a spouse who is disrespectful to him or her. A celebrity is pulled over by the police and treated like a criminal. A person who has tons of money in the bank has his wallet and identity stolen and is, for half a day, literally poor. A high-powered business executive can't get her first-grader to get in the car.

Remember that there was a time when the sun never set on the British Empire. Before that, the Portuguese and Spanish had global hegemony. The Chinese had their dynasties, and the Mongols at one time created the largest contiguous land empire the world has ever known. At times, the most influential empires were in the Middle East, like the Arab conquests, Persia, and Babylonia. In the early fourteenth century, the world's richest man was in Timbuktu, in the African Mali Empire. The Inca Empire extended for 2,500 miles in South America before the Europeans came and established dominance.

But everything changes, and all power is fleeting. No matter when, where, or who, there will come a time when we get sick, grow old, and lose power. Death is ultimately on top, and we always end up one-down.

THE PRACTICE

1. In what situations do you feel one-up? Why?
2. In what situations do you feel one-down? Why?
3. In what situations do you notice the one-up/one-down status shifting?
4. In what situations do you notice freedom from one-up/one-down dynamics?

12   *Talking about Social Privilege*

I acknowledge the privilege of being alive in a human body
at this moment, endowed with senses, memories, emotions,
thoughts, and the space of mind in its wisdom aspect.

—Alex Grey, "The Vast Expanse"

"You girls are so lucky." Kim's mum would say this often to Kim and her
sister when they were growing up in Southeast Asia. "Just think, if you
had been born in another country, you might be a maid doing someone else's housework. Or if you had been born in China not long ago,
you might have been left by the river to die, especially you, Kim. They
didn't want any girls, least of all a Tiger girl like you. Nobody would have
wanted that trouble!"

At times, Kim's mother spoke these words lightly and playfully. But
at other times she was sharp and latently accusative. In either mood her
meaning was abundantly clear: Kim and her sister led lives of significant
privilege, and they should never forget it. She was referring to the fact
that they were born legally in the United Kingdom; they spoke English;
they were in good health; and they benefited from social systems that

shielded them from the fate of having to do manual labor, or even worse, infanticide.

When Kim was about sixteen she moved back to the UK. While studying for her exams that year she realized that she had begun to understand her mum's admonitions. She was now keenly aware of the privileges her mother had harped on over the years, and it had changed the way she felt about school. She found herself studying harder than ever before—a sharp change from the girl who had once resented school, rebelled, and resisted her teachers.

Now she found herself thinking about girls in Southeast and Far East Asia who were much less privileged than her, girls who might not have the choice to continue to go to school. She thought about what that meant for their future opportunities and the compromises they had to make, like working in a foreign country to send money home to their children. She saw how even the freedom to choose subjects in school was a kind of luxury. To be able to pick from the arts, biology, or sociology based on her own interests was both a pleasure and a privilege. Kim began to see her studies, learning, and the fulfillment of her potential as a way to embody her own privilege and to be accountable to it. She didn't want to waste the opportunities she had been given—opportunities, as her mum pointed out, that she enjoyed simply by virtue of being born into certain life circumstances.

What Is Social Privilege?

The word *privilege* is defined as a right or immunity granted as a particular benefit, advantage, or favor. In common parlance it refers to all the ways we enjoy certain advantages in life that others may not have. There are an endless number of privileges that we relish. Some are shared, while others are very particular and unique to each of us. Sometimes we are highly aware of our privileges; other times we take them for granted.

We typically think of good looks, extra money, attending elite schools, and a membership at the country club as forms of privilege. We ascribe privilege to being white, male, straight, cisgendered, wealthy, or from the Northern or the Western hemispheres. These sweeping categories contain broad truths, but privilege also comes in forms other than socioeconomic status.

For example, privilege could derive from a God-given talent for mathematics or music or language. Or it could come in the form of a learned skill set. Knowing your way around a kitchen because of your epicurean mother might be a real advantage when looking for work in the restaurant business. Maybe it's an emotional capacity that you didn't have to work for—perhaps you grew up in a family that shared feelings easily, talked about issues, and remained close even through difficult times, so you left home with a natural sense of belonging and social ease. You might not think of yourself as privileged, but compared to someone who had a lot of emotional distress at home, your circumstances are far more favorable for being able to sustain long-term relationships. People don't tend to think of spirituality as a form of privilege, but a deep immersion in matters of ultimate concern provides sanctuary and respite when times get tough. There is certainly privilege in that.

Like Kim's mum, we can think in terms of the privileges that our social systems afford us. How about free public education, or the ability to own property, save money, or have a bank account that cannot lawfully be taken away? How about being able to cast a vote in a free election? Or the freedom to pick up and move to another state, with no interference from anyone else? That's not the case in many parts of the world. If you enjoy any of these advantages, you are more privileged than many others.

The discussion of social privilege may have begun with the American sociologist and historian W. E. B. Du Bois and his 1904 collection of essays, *The Souls of Black Folk*. He wrote that although black Americans were observant of white Americans and conscious of racial discrimination, white Americans did not think that much about black Americans, nor about the effects of racial discrimination. He later described the kinds of advantages that the white populace enjoyed by simply being white that were denied to black people. Common courtesy, polite treatment, admission to public functions and places, lenient treatment in the court system, and access to the best schools were examples of what he called the "public and psychological wages" afforded to whites, what today we call "white privilege."[1] Du Bois invited us to look at our social context and recognize these profound differences. We begin to see how most social identities—those of economic class, religion, sexual orientation, or gender identity—afford advantages or deny them.

Blind to Privilege

There is an old American saying that refers to having social privilege but not knowing it. It's often attributed to a college football coach, Barry Switzer, but apparently it goes back even earlier,[2] to a baseball metaphor that goes like this: "Some people are born on third base and go through life thinking they hit a triple." The implication is that we enjoy and benefit from our privilege, as though we have earned it. It could be that we just don't think about it, or maybe we really believe that we earned it. Or maybe it's such a common feature of our life that we can't get a perspective on it. It's the water we swim in, and like a fish, we're never separate from it. Or maybe we've never thought about our circumstances compared to those of others, so the contrast fails to get our attention. The point is that social privilege ensures that we don't have to think about it. To use Du Bois's example again, people of color have to relate to racial discrimination constantly, while white people are free to ignore it.

It takes some thought to recognize privilege, which is why some parents remind their kids of it all the time. Kim's mum wanted her daughters to appreciate the benefits they have in life and notice the many things they enjoy that are not automatically afforded to everyone. In learning to appreciate her own circumstances, Kim naturally began to consider the circumstances of others: the young girls who, unlike her, didn't have access to school or education. She started to think about them on *their* terms, and as she did, the reality of their lives became even more vivid to her. She began to include their perspectives, life challenges, and suffering in her outlook on the world.

Because privilege can blind us to the reality of others' lived experience, we often remain oblivious to their struggles. Short of living with illness or disability, we might go for an entire lifetime without considering the rising cost of insulin for a diabetic, the extreme challenge of traveling for a person in a wheelchair, or the sustained difficulty of raising a child with autism. We might fail to acknowledge the anxiety a transgender person may experience when their personal sense of gender is not reflected back to them by others, or understand the relief of a nonbinary or gender-queer person when they don't have to fix their gender identity by checking the box as male or female. We might fail to acknowledge the daily struggles of being an immigrant or a person trying to live on a minimum wage. Learning to recognize and talk about privilege is a form of compassion that opens the mind and awakens the heart to others whose circumstances are different from our own.

Social privilege is a global phenomenon as well as a local one. For example, a position in the north of the global economy permits us to buy a bar of chocolate in San Francisco or an iPhone in London without having to consider the controversies of the production and distribution of these products. Issues regarding child labor, human rights violations, and exploitation of natural resources are rife in the production of cacao[3] on the Ivory Coast and in the mining industry in Central Africa,[4] but as affluent people in the West, we are shielded from knowing about these issues. Kwame Anthony Appiah, a British-born, Ghanaian-American philosopher and cultural theorist, writes about the importance of expanding the range of our ethical concerns to include people in other parts of the world.[5] This expansion of our awareness to others around the globe is an act of compassion, an opening of the heart to include others.

Talking about Privilege

Social privilege often results from unjust social practices, and it can blind us to that very injustice. In other words, when we are privileged we simply can't see the problem. This makes talking about privilege difficult. Conversations often can become confrontational or blaming when some people demand that others recognize their own privilege. The atmosphere can become hostile, and people easily become defensive when asked to "check your privilege." Sometimes people are told that they are "too privileged" to have a valid perspective, which can result in their withdrawal from the interaction.

Privilege is difficult to acknowledge for lots of reasons, first, because some forms of privilege highlight deep historical injustices, as Du Bois points out. Despite our great advances toward equality, we are reminded that some groups of people have been treated unfairly for centuries, and these systemic patterns are still in place. As Dr. Martin Luther King Jr. said, "Injustice anywhere is a threat to justice everywhere."[6] It's not easy for any of us to be confronted with the truth that we may be benefiting from a legacy that has harmed others.

Another reason privilege is difficult to acknowledge is because it generates feelings of guilt, sorrow, shame, or helplessness. Kim remembers an uncomfortable early memory while traveling through India with her family when she was about eight years old. She and her sister were expressing sympathy for the street animals that looked starved and diseased, when her mum remarked, "It's interesting that you don't say that about the children, only the animals." The two sisters looked at each other, feeling both awkward and guilty, not knowing what to say, much less what to do. Their helplessness weighed heavily on their young minds, particularly since they would continue on with their travels, while the children's circumstances would, most likely, never change. Guilt arises because even though we can acknowledge the advantages in our lives, the question of what to do for others remains a quandary.

Recognizing and Using Our Privilege

Including discussions of privilege in conversation can be enriching and revealing. Acknowledging privilege provides a basis for gratitude, for the recognition of others unlike ourselves, and is an opportunity for deepening generosity and grace. It's not about proving how "woke" someone is, dominating others into taking a certain worldview or manipulating conversation to get people to do what we want. It's about showing up responsibly, with humility, and expanding how we think, feel and, most importantly, act in the world.

The three of us had an unfortunate experience recently. We were part of an online conference in which an array of different teachers gave presentations on conflict-resolution skills. There was one session in which two experienced teachers gave a presentation on diversity that included a discussion of the wisdom of Native cultures vis-à-vis conflict. One teacher was a Polynesian male, and one was a Native American female; both were people of color. At one point, a white male participant interrupted the woman teacher in the middle of her presentation. He said that he was disappointed because from his perspective everyone already understood the content of her teaching, that it was too basic. He went on to say that he was bored and that he would prefer that she focus on some other topic of more interest to him.

It was painful to witness. First of all, he was straight-up rude. Second, he displayed a stark example of unconscious privilege. We imagine that if you would ask him, he would say that his interruption and comments had nothing to do with race or gender. But from the outside it was impossible to disregard the scene of a white male interrupting a woman of color, dissing her presentation and behaving as though she was obligated to please him. He felt entitled to assert himself in this way and was, at the same time, oblivious to its impact. It would have been less painful if it were just a case of bad manners, but the interplay of race and gender was too glaring to overlook, and an onlooker had little choice but to see the misuse of white male privilege.[7]

To their credit, the two teachers remained receptive to his complaints. In this they demonstrated mature eldership. They listened to his perspective and accorded him the respect he failed to extend to them. Luckily, in a breakout session, another mature participant gave the man some feedback on how his interruption had negatively affected him, and that he didn't agree with his complaint at all. By framing his feedback in terms of his own personal experience, this man managed to refrain from patronizing the woman teacher and in so doing, indirectly supported her leadership. In this way he modeled how to use one's privilege positively—by using his communication skills to give direct, thoughtful feedback to the man in a way that he could hear and receive.

The most important takeaway from any discussion about privilege is to see that we can use our privilege for the benefit of others in less advantaged positions. In the context of conversation, using privilege could simply be a willingness to listen openly to someone else's pain or frustration. It could be in the form of offering feedback to someone who is less skilled or self-aware, as we saw in the previous example. It could come in the form of asking genuine, thoughtful questions and reflecting on the responses. Or it could be a willingness to challenge others, helping them overcome their biases to assist them in developing their strength of character.

We can leverage our privilege for the benefit of others in all kinds of ways. One example of the positive use of male privilege comes from our Zen practice. Diane acknowledges that sometimes it can be difficult to be a woman in leadership, particularly a teacher of Zen. She sometime finds it challenging to impose the discipline of the Zen tradition, with its rigorous forms and explicit hierarchy, particularly in a culture like America, which places tremendous value on each individual and his or her preferences and opinions.

Recently, she began to notice that in certain contexts her leadership role was easier to fulfill. She seemed to have fewer power struggles with students, with far less testing of her in her role as teacher or leader. She began to wonder about this. One day it occurred to her that her oldest and most committed student, Rob McNamara, was almost always present in the situations in which she was able to hold her leadership more lightly. She realized that Rob used his male privilege to support a woman in a position of leadership. She saw how he modeled for other students that a strong male can receive guidance from a woman. He further showed how a student can orient to a teacher without compromising his or her dignity. He did this quietly, consistently, and almost invisibly, quite possibly without consciously or explicitly trying to model to others. Diane has grown to really appreciate the experience of a male using his privilege to support her in her role.

This Precious Human Birth

The historical Buddha was born into privilege. He was the son of a king and raised with endless riches and pleasures of all kinds. He was twenty-nine when he ventured outside the walls of his palace, and like Kim, he saw people far less fortunate than himself: a sick person, an old man, and a corpse. When he realized that his privileged status would not protect him from encounters with sickness, old age, and death, he was shaken to his core.[8] This began the start of his spiritual quest. Through the potency of his intention to awaken and his rigorous commitment to meditation, the Buddha saw through the relative conditions of this life. Conventional categories of one-up/one-down, rich and poor, privileged and disadvantaged were social conditions only. He saw beyond them to the innate dignity and preciousness of all beings regardless of status. In Zen he is called "A True Person of No Rank." This is the fundamental realization that our labels, our prejudices, and even our deeply held ideas about what constitutes fortune and misfortune don't hold up; every living being is equally precious, regardless of their conditions and circumstances.

True value derives from life itself, from the conditions of "this precious human birth." This phrase comes from the Chiggala Sutra, where the Buddha speaks about the rare circumstances of being born human.[9] He likens it to a blind sea turtle swimming in a vast ocean in which someone has tossed an ox yoke with a hole in the center. And every one hundred years the turtle surfaces. The Buddha says our chances of being born human are the same as those of the turtle surfacing with his head in the center of the yoke—very rare indeed. And given how rare, how inherently precious our life is.

We swim in a vast ocean of privilege, as Alex Grey, a visionary artist, author, and Buddhist teacher, points out; this is because we are alive, because we have "senses, memories, emotions, thoughts, and most importantly, the space of mind in its wisdom aspect."[10] It is a privilege to write this book, to have conversation, and to participate in awakening to see ourselves and others as fundamentally worthy, even as we inhabit our relative differences and work to create fair and just conditions for all people in this precious life.

THE PRACTICE

1. Think of a group of people in society who land in a less privileged category. Spend some time doing some research about the challenges they face and notice your emotional responses or ability to empathize. Be guided by the question, "What is it like to be them?

2. Think of an occasion where you felt uncomfortable about your privilege. How could you have used your privilege in a way that supported others?

13   *Politically Correct*

The truth has become an insult.
—Chimamanda Ngozi Adichie, *Half of a Yellow Sun*

You're not going to believe this. We may have experienced the most politically incorrect moment in the twenty-first century. First of all, this took place in Berkeley, California, the beating heart and soul of American liberalism. We were leading a workshop with a wonderful cross-section of people: Bay Area social justice activists, executives from Silicon Valley, Northern California consciousness types, and tech people from up and down the peninsula. There were Asians and Hispanics, black people, white people, and mixed people. There were Jews and gentiles, Buddhists, New Age types, and atheists. There were males, females, and gender-diverse people. Even the age range was wide, from those born with a cell phone in their hand, to those who still ask for help every time they boot up a computer. It was an extravaganza of diversity.

Our intention was to share some of our humble skills with this woke and varied group. So the first morning we set up a conversation with about eight people to demonstrate and practice a few simple things. We took a few minutes for introductions, to establish gender pronouns, and to ask people to give a little bit of context for why they were at the workshop. Pretty straightforward, no?

Everything was going swimmingly, that is, until one young man, eighteen years old, introduced himself as "a black woman." His skin was white, and his manner didn't convey fluidity, but that's what he said: "My name is John, and I am a black woman." When he spoke, the world came to an abrupt halt. Birds in the sky stopped flying, and fish in the sea quit swimming, and everyone in the room quit breathing, especially Diane, who was facilitating. There were so many problems with what had just happened, but she couldn't name them because her mind went totally blank. She was completely stunned. It was such a strange experience that she wasn't sure that it was politically incorrect—it was just wrong and weird. But we will come back to this story later . . .

What Is PC?

Political correctness, PC, is commonly understood to mean making efforts to avoid offense to groups or individuals, especially those who have been and are marginalized. It can involve avoiding stereotypes or pejorative language. It involves paying more attention to power relationships and attempting to accord respect to everyone. The term came into common parlance in the 1970s and is sometimes mocked because certain people react negatively to any constraints on their speech. But political correctness, or paying attention to our language so that it's not disrespectful to others, is a worthy effort. It wakes us up to the impact of our words. It alerts us to negative stereotypes; it insists that we cut out crude racist and sexist jokes. It reveals our biases, and it challenges us to be more fundamentally aware when we're talking to and about others.

There probably isn't a reader among us who hasn't been caught perpetuating a stereotype, sometimes unwittingly, or telling a joke at the expense of someone else. It's never easy when you're expressing yourself freely, especially if you think you're being funny, to be met with a scowl, a frown, or a furrowed brow and be told that you're being inappropriate.

But political correctness isn't just about bad jokes. It's about warding off the great damage people do with their words, from denigrating and injuring others, to creating tension, division, and even inciting violence between groups of people. In the Buddha's teaching of the Noble Eightfold Path, right speech is one of the fundamental practices that lead us off the wheel of suffering to liberation.[1] This is because words shape our perceptions, influence our minds, and form the basis of our actions.

The United States has always made a strong distinction between speech and actions, protecting freedom of speech, preserving the right to express views within certain limits, and ensuring that the government doesn't suppress open expression. Nonetheless, negative thoughts lead to harmful language, and harmful language usually prepares the ground for destructive actions. So we have to be careful, because our thoughts, speech, and actions reinforce one another. This is also true for kind thoughts, respectful words, and beneficial actions.

Political correctness is a form of right speech. It is truly remarkable for a culture to collectively attempt to change negative habits in real time. Nowadays, PC values have taken on such momentum that nearly everyone is compelled to participate—journalists, politicians, managers, athletes, celebrities—even when they don't want to. And if they don't want to, at least they have to think long and hard about why not.

But the people who are offended by PC culture also have a point. They find it excessive or dogmatic, and they rail against the self-righteousness of it. They resent incidents of hypersensitivity and fear that we conflate individual emotional troubles with victimization from society. We may think we're giving support to victims, but we may just be catering to a particular person's narcissistic whims. Sometimes people use political correctness to assert their own egos, to power trip or lord it over others. Other times they interfere with the "free pursuit of ideas and open knowledge."[2] This can be a real problem. Comedians in particular are bothered by interference with free speech.[3] George Carlin once said, "Political correctness is America's newest form of intolerance, and it's especially pernicious because it comes disguised as tolerance."[4] Another comedian called it "recreational outrage."[5] Many comedians won't even play colleges anymore because students are prone to being offended.

In the interpersonal space that we three work in, there is a tremendous upside to people being mindful of their speech and its impact. Everyone becomes more aware, inclusive, and respectful of all people. Difficult conversations flow much more smoothly when everyone in the room feels respected and knows that there's a place for their personal perspective. On the other hand, extreme political correctness creates an environment of hypervigilance, a feeling of walking on eggshells. Participants withdraw from conversation, refusing to take risks for fear of making mistakes. This is the very definition of a poor learning environment. Another problem, too, is that people who make PC assertions, reprimands, and corrections often assume that there is only one perspective or truth that will cover complex situations. And we all know that isn't the case. Take the following example:

Diane was facilitating a conversation about the problem of sexual harassment and the rise of the #MeToo movement. The group met online and was exchanging opinions about these trends in culture. There were several men who declined to contribute to the conversation, even though they had joined the online forum. When she asked them about their thoughts on the matter, they refused to jump in because they said they believed they were not able to speak freely and could only agree with the perspectives already held by the others in the group. As much as Diane prodded them to express their points of view, they remained firm. They weren't angry or resentful. They were just unwilling to say anything. This was an enormous loss to the conversation, because when it comes to clarifying sexual dynamics, we all need to learn from one another. There are just too many situations that don't fall into neat categories.

Diane lamented the fact that these emotionally mature men with real opinions were refusing to engage in conversation. So she gave the group members a challenge and pressed on, inviting everyone to overcome the perceived intolerance in the forum. She reminded them to practice being for each other and to entertain multiple perspectives, seeing how every perspective is both true and partial.

With that, she facilitated the themes that everyone could agree on. In this group there was tremendous support for #MeToo and for sexual misconduct being brought into the open and dealt with. They wanted to acknowledge the prevalence of sexual assault and abuse in our culture and to recognize how devastating it can be for survivors, particularly when they are silenced. They concurred that too many people for too long have been sexually assaulted or abused, and when they finally build up the courage to report it to family or authorities, they are doubted, blamed, or ignored. Everyone was relieved that these issues were being addressed in public forums, online, and in the press. As a society, we seem to be maturing by finally listening to victims and taking action to stop predators and abusers from doing more harm.

Once the sameness between forum members was established, they wandered into more dangerous territory by exploring their differences. Some wanted to recognize a broad spectrum of sexual misconduct and make better distinctions between what's crude, distasteful, or creepy, and what constitutes actual sexual harassment or is downright criminal. Some were concerned about the tendency for a public reaction to an accusation of inappropriate sexual behavior to be disproportionate to the actual offense. Others were concerned with a lack of proportionality and due process for alleged offenders, particularly when social media becomes judge and jury.[6] They began to wonder aloud about what men's and women's respective responsibilities are in terms of clarifying intentions and communicating them. They questioned why men don't do more to educate younger men about these issues. They expressed concern that women could stand to lose power by relying on men, instead of setting the tone, terms, and conditions of their sexual encounters. They weren't agreeing with one another, but they were speaking freely, listening and creating room for many perspectives.[7]

The most potent, dynamic part of the conversation regarded consent when engaging in sexual activity. They described their own successes and failures in relation to consent, revealing vulnerability, confusion, and some regret. The group deepened their bond by sharing incidents of their own mistakes, and gained clarity about the skill of eliciting clear agreements in their sexual engagements. Learning to say or hear "yes" without ambivalence and to express or receive "no" without anxiety was a theme that interested everyone.

By overcoming the barrier to speaking freely, this group was able to look more closely at their own motives for engaging erotically, including the challenge of mixing desire and ambition. They all acknowledged how often they'd been hurt and how many times they had hurt others. Everyone was interested in more self-responsibility and better communication. In the end, it was a dynamic, satisfying conversation in which both men and women fully participated, and the forum ended with everyone having something to think about.

How do we include the respect and grace of the intention of political correctness without succumbing to its potential for judgment and oppression? By using the same skill set that we set forth throughout this book. Here are some of the keys:

Listening

Listening is key to all good communication. The problem is that we think we are great listeners until we hear something that isn't consistent with our current thinking. Then we become tense, contracted, and defensive, and the conversation fails to expand into new territory. In an atmosphere of political correctness this is even more true because listening is often replaced by a compliant form of silence, which isn't listening at all. To counter that, we have to calm ourselves down in the face of disagreement, and even when it's uncomfortable, when we don't like it, we must try to sincerely listen for the partial truth in what's being said. Good listening always involves emptying out, becoming present, receiving the message, and reflecting back what we've heard. Remember that listening doesn't equal agreement. To reflect back a message that we don't agree with is an excellent practice in creating space in our mind for multiple perspectives. Listening supports all good conversations, whether in the office, at home, or having drinks with friends.

True and Partial

Once we're able to calm down and listen to an opinion that differs from our own, we can take the next step and look for a partial truth. Asking the question "What's right about what's being said?" is a good start. Ken Wilber is fond of saying that no one can be 100 percent right all the time, nor can someone be 100 percent wrong.[8] He reminds us to build our capacity to include multiple perspectives in the space of an open mind.

The challenge is very similar to the difficulty we face in listening. When fight or flight is aroused, we literally lose our capacity to entertain multiple perspectives because our attention narrows for a quick, defensive response. We lose our ability to hold complexity, nuance, or contradictions, and instead our thinking becomes very black-and-white. So it's important to practice when we feel calm because it's much easier to see different points of view as each having some validity.

A friend had a delicate situation in a group he was coaching. A man in the group shared that he works in a consulting company where seven out of ten employees are women, one of whom is the CEO. They have an agreement to bring their conflicts out into the open and to practice communicating directly. But apparently they don't do that very well. In a moment of frustration, he said to the other members of the coaching group, some of whom were women, that the dynamics in his company reminded him of a "clique of girls in junior high school." He was immediately called out for being sexist by another member of the group. This led to a spontaneous debate about whether he was or wasn't. But before the conversation quickly went off the rails, our friend, the facilitator, simply asked everyone to slow down. First, he helped the group see that what appeared sexist in this man's speech was two things: characterizing his female coworkers essentially as silly, immature young girls—a put-down, and, maybe to a lesser degree, one that invokes a negative stereotype of young teenage girls.

This clarification helped relax the group. Then our friend supported the man by saying, "If we get rid of the put-down and the stereotype, there is something true in what you are experiencing. What exactly is the behavior you don't like?" The man replied that issues are not brought out directly, and that people talk negatively behind one another's backs. He felt hurt by this. The facilitator empathized with him and agreed that those behaviors are painful and dysfunctional. He then praised the man for wanting to change the dynamics and for seeking guidance from the group for how to do so. The accusation of sexism was dispelled, and the group proceeded to address his original concerns.

Intention vs. Impact

When we run into moments in conversation that either offend or oppress us, we often assume that we know the intentions of others. But since intentions are subjective, we can't really know what they are without asking. In the excellent book *Difficult Conversations: How to Discuss What Matters Most*, the authors Douglas Stone, Bruce Patton, and Sheila Heen, who teach at Harvard Law School and the Harvard Negotiation Project, make a very important distinction between intention and impact. They assert that we can feel a negative impact, and without minimizing it, not presume a negative intention. And then we may find our way to a clarification or resolution that we didn't expect.[9]

So now is the time to return to the story that started this chapter:

"My name is John, and I am a black woman."

After a long pause, Diane looked to two black women sitting in the circle. One was a young trans woman, not yet thirty, and the other woman was about fifty years old. Diane said, "Would you like to respond to what you just heard?"

Both were eager to respond. The younger woman simply said to him, "Nah. Because if you were a black woman, you would know better than to say something crazy like what you just said."

The older woman followed: "I don't know your meaning here, but when you say that you are a black woman, it's baffling to me. We black people have just claimed our space and voice, especially black women.

So when you say that the impact on you is negative, I feel *our* place, *our* voice, and *our* unique experiences are being taken again. I'm pretty sure that isn't what you want to have happen."

They could have responded with contempt, but they were both real, generous, and surprisingly tolerant of the young man's inexperience.

But the young man began to double down and reassert himself, saying that he meant that he *feels* like a black woman on the inside.

Diane interrupted him. "I have an idea about what would be really helpful here. What if you started by simply repeating back what you heard them say? Would you be willing to do that first?"

He relented and quietly agreed. So he did—he repeated exactly what he had heard the two woman say, and he did a pretty good job. In the process, he became very tender and vulnerable. Remember, he was only eighteen. His whole demeanor changed, from someone who was awkwardly asserting himself to someone who had begun to open up and listen. Both of the women were very kind to him in their responses, thanking him for reflecting their words accurately and hearing what they each had to say.

Diane then turned to him and said, "You know, I'm not entirely sure what you intended, either." She was wondering if she could find any partial truth in his wildly provocative statement. "It seems like you were trying to empathize or create some sort of connection. Is that the case?"

He nodded yes.

Diane said, "I'm wondering if you feel connected now?"

He nodded again.

"Can you see how you created that connection through listening rather than through asserting yourself?"

"Yes."

"Did you also notice how you succeeded because you were interested in *their* experience, in *their* differences from you, instead of imagining you're the same?"

"Right," he said, nodding again. He seemed to get it. By now he had fully relaxed, as had everyone else.

Then Diane praised him. "It is good to empathize and to want connection with others. I appreciate you for hanging in there in this conversation. Then she turned to the two women and the other members of the group. "Thank you for being so real and so engaged." And then she turned to the young man with a wink: "Hey, don't ever say you're a black woman again."

THE PRACTICE

The objective is to cultivate flexibility of mind by finding the partial truth in a statement you don't agree with. Find a willing partner to practice with.

1. Sit facing each other in a comfortable upright position. Close your eyes and breathe, settling your nervous system.
2. Each of you will take turns expressing a viewpoint, one not shared by the other. The listener simply receives the statement and notices the impact it has on their physiology.
3. Then the listener becomes the speaker and reflects the viewpoint just expressed, emphasizing what is valid about it. In other words, the speaker reflects on the *partial truth* in the other person's perspective.

14 *Growing through Conflict*

When I let go of what I am, I become what I might be.
— John Heider and Lao Tzu, *The Tao of Leadership*

Conflict is difficult, but it can be useful. When we clash with others it heightens our attention, exposes our perspectives, and highlights where we need to grow. Fighting with a family member about our personal beliefs reveals what we really think and feel. Withdrawing from the religion of our youth, something that often stirs up conflict, allows us to ask our real existential questions. Aggressive political debates, while tense, particularly when there is no apparent compromise, disclose the deeply held values of both sides. Uncomfortable as they are, these conflicts are a tremendous source of wisdom, showing us how much we care, and at the same time, how limited our views are, regardless of our certainty about them. We have to remember that all perspectives are true, but partial. As soon as we can see this, we can begin to expand our viewpoints.

A few years ago, Kim remembers sitting in a bar in Berlin with an old school friend, George, who was squabbling with his older brother, Will. The argument was about whether Will was actually present at a party they were reminiscing about.

"You weren't there!" accused George. "You always do this—you insert yourself into other people's memories," he teased.

"No, that's not true," said Will. "I was definitely there! I totally remember it."

Will's energetic response matched George's vigor, then he looked to Kim as if to convince her that his perspective was true. George elbowed Will away as he leaned in, looking Kim straight in the eye, insisting, "Kim, don't listen to him; he's not right. My story is the *real* truth."

The brothers pushed each other around and laughed it off. It was funny, but also revealing to hear what they were saying.

Conflict is an indication that either side of an argument is pretending to be the whole story. Robert Kegan, a developmental psychologist and research professor at Harvard, explains it this way: "Conflict is a likely consequence of one or both of us making prior, true, distinct, and whole our partial position . . . a reminder of our tendency to pretend to completeness when we are, in fact, incomplete. We may have this conflict because we need it to recover our truer complexity."[1]

We can decide to be curious about our conflicts, to expand our perspectives and try on new viewpoints. We come to realize that the Truth, with a capital *T*, is always bigger than we can see from our personal vantage point. We also have an opportunity to reach a more subtle, inclusive understanding and discover humility in the process.

A friend of ours, Amy, shared how within her family the Catholic faith has been both a binding force and a painful divider. Her younger sister, who identifies as queer, naturally has concerns about Catholicism's treatment of homosexuality. In contrast, Amy has reconnected with her Catholic faith in recent years, despite having rejected it as a teenager. While it has been difficult for them to navigate through this together, by practicing thoughtful listening and refusing to be personally offended, they have come to a more nuanced peace with their differences. They recognize that they can each hold contrasting views about the church and its institutional policies while still acknowledging the spiritual guidance valued by many of its members, including Amy. And all the while they continue to love and respect each other as sisters.

Conflict is also a driver of social change. Amy's sister may well be right, and the Catholic Church may change its position regarding homosexuality in time. The social progression toward the abolition of slavery, giving women and minority groups the right to vote, and introducing rights for children and people with disabilities all signify a trend toward greater inclusion and fairness.[2] It has been said that "there is nothing more powerful than an idea whose time has come."[3] Yet how we get there, how we move through conflicts that are presently unsolvable, is the challenging question.

Coming Together, Falling Apart

According to research, approximately 60 percent of all human conflicts around the world center on identity and culture.[4] Identity is one of our most prized possessions, something we hold tightly to. Sometimes identity leads to surprising eruptions of conflict that suddenly reveal hidden divisions. In 2016, the United Kingdom held a referendum on whether to leave or stay in the European Union. The vote was extremely close in favor of leaving, and many people were stunned by this outcome. Residents of London, who identify as British but are amenable to Europe, had to acknowledge how blind they had been to the views held by the rest of the country. Outside of London, people thought of themselves as Brits exclusively—a far more nationalistic identity. It was an opportunity for constructive conversations about this difference in identity, as well as the economic implications of the decision to leave the European Union, but that didn't happen. In its absence, powerful ethnocentrism came to dominate the discourse, and the debate became much more divisive and hostile.[5]

While attending university in Brighton, England, Kim was part of a conflict that centered around identity. She belonged to a political action group that came together for an intense period to share in political solidarity and friendship despite differences in their identities. In early 2009, over fifty students gathered on campus to protest the Gaza War. At the time there were many universities in the UK that were engaging in similar coordinated protests. A smaller group of about thirty students set up

an occupation in one of the larger lecture halls to protest, demanding a response from the university administration. Students camped out, creating
their own temporary community, from arranging town hall meetings and
task force groups, to organizing cooked meals for everyone, to construct-
ing a makeshift space they could live in. Very quickly, issues of privilege
and inequality rose up among individuals, accompanied by intense critical
analysis of themselves along the lines of race, sex, and class. People were
enlivened, gripped both in their activity of working toward a common
committed cause while confronting inequities within their own coalition.

The protest concluded after successfully negotiating an agreement
with the university administration. For a while, a small core group of students stayed tightly woven into one another's lives, celebrating their win,
their diversity, and their togetherness. The levels of care they showed one
another was touching. They offered support in many ways, even tackling
personal problems like homelessness, trauma, and identity issues that
had previously been kept private.

Soon, however, ominous rifts began to appear between individuals in
this core group. People formed alliances and started to take strong stands
with one another regarding their views, speech, and expressions of identity. They began designating what kinds of behaviors and speech were
and were not acceptable. Little by little, the group splintered. Some people discreetly drifted away, while others left after intensely personal fights
and excruciating confrontations. Many felt loss and tragedy in what had
happened, including Kim.

Later, she reflected that one of the significant lessons for her was in
the shift from their common political cause, where for a while their diversity was a source of energy and power. But when the protest ended, so
did their solidarity, and they disintegrated into their individual identities, serving their own agendas and nursing their personal traumas and
unhealed wounds. They migrated from an ethnocentric identity, bound
by a common cause and a clear sense of *us* and *them*, to their egocentric
differences. These then became insurmountable. Goodwill was lost, and
mild suspicion quickly grew into mistrust and eventually exile. The group
wasn't able to use their conflicts to grow and learn, and unfortunately, it

fractured in the end. Many friendships dissolved, and people went away hurt and confused.

Fighting for an important issue brings us together as long as the "other" is outside our own group. But when those same dynamics persist within the group, it becomes very destructive. That's why it's so important to learn to work with conflict. We can certainly fight the good fight when necessary, but we can also refrain from habitual patterns of competition, contentiousness, and aggression when they don't serve.

It's not easy to rework these patterns and rewire our responses. The physiological, mental, and energetic stress can make leaning into conflict a highly counterintuitive move. And yet, it is only through our relationships, building up more stamina and willingness to navigate the discomfort together, that we can harness the creative potential of conflict to propel our own and our collective growth. There are certain keys to dealing with conflict that can help us navigate the fear and discomfort so that we may stay engaged enough to create a positive outcome.

Attending to the Body

Let's recall that to work constructively with conflict, we must make a new relationship with the body. The fight-or-flight response is intense and disruptive, and managing the sensations that arise from adrenalin and cortisol takes practice. Often our habitual response to conflict is a coping mechanism that, when we pay closer attention, doesn't help us solve our problem. Fighting can help us express the intensity of our experience while staying engaged; cope with the dysregulation in the body; and withdrawal can give us a break, but the problem persists. Eventually, we have to find a way to calm down, restore relaxation to the body and mind, and negotiate our wants and needs.

Identifying difficult sensations, being present to them and using the breath to calm the system, is something we should repeat often. Over time, the sensations become less scary and overwhelming, and we develop a sense of when the body is disrupted and when it's harmonized. We learn about the flavors of our emotional states and can recognize when the mind is open and available, and when we're using its resources for attack and defense, creating deeper problems for ourselves.

As we said earlier, when we are triggered, our cognition is impeded and our interpersonal skills are impaired. It becomes almost impossible to express ourselves coherently and listen well. Under these circumstances we usually experience only a single truth, and we compulsively argue for it. We literally cannot entertain another perspective, and it's difficult to experience our allegiances as real.

Since fight or flight compromises our skills, it's very important that we calm down first and then practice turn-taking in our communications. When the nervous system is calm, listening is far easier. When emotions abate, we can hold multiple views. When the mind settles down, we remember that we are committed to one another's well-being. In other words, by regulating our nervous system, we can more easily remember that we are for each other.

Building and Sustaining Connection

In Kim's story, her group was very successful at galvanizing around a common cause to mount a protest against the Gaza War and the associated human rights violations. But the members of the group continued to push for their principles and ideals within the group to the point that it became divisive. This can happen when we don't have a powerful understanding of the relationship of sameness to difference. If people had wanted their friendships to continue, they would have had to spend considerable time building connection and rapport, deepening their bonds and affirming their appreciation of one another, even as they explored issues of power, privilege, and identity. Instead, they challenged one another's views, speech, and behaviors. They began to mistrust their own social structures, criticizing those in power for how they expressed or used it. While they attempted to be inclusive, they began excluding one another in communications, which had become dogmatic and defensive. Pretty soon the entire environment was stressful. People started to build coalitions, breaking off from others into small groups.

Over time, as the collective sense of goodwill and friendship continued to erode, growing together was no longer an option. The group could not recover from the conflicts, as differences ruled the day. Some of the most well-intended political movements become victims to identity politics like this. In retrospect, Kim appreciated their time advocating together but was saddened by the lost opportunity to continue their friendships, working with their values, differences, and conflicts in a more constructive way.

Flexible Identity

Since identity is such a common source of conflict, it serves us to consciously notice when, why, and how much we rely on identity. Keep in mind that we have many different identities, all of which can serve and support our work and relationships.

But too much attachment to identity can also create separation and suffering. We may habitually behave as an advocate when being a friend is better. We may stand up for our racial or gender differences when acknowledging our common humanity creates more calm, ease, and connection. We may identify with the suffering of the past when the present moment is filled with beauty and substance. Or we may identify with the fighter in us when the peacemaker is who's needed.

Paulo Freire, a highly influential Brazilian educator, argued that without a sense of identity there can be no real struggle.[6] On the other hand, when we hold too tightly to our identity we also create struggle. It's important to remember that identity can be flexible, and we can shift identity in the midst of conflict, as well as relax it altogether.

Determination

The Dalai Lama tells us, "If you become discouraged, that is the real failure; you have lost a valuable chance to develop. To remain determined is itself a gain."[7] Growing through conflict is no easy feat. Having difficult conversations can be frustrating, awkward, energy sapping, and risky. We will be confronted with the truth that our perspective is limited and bi-ased, and our growth depends on being open to changing what we think, how we feel, and how we see the world.

People have a tendency when thinking of their extreme adversary to throw up their hands: "It's just not worth it. There's no talking to them." But there's a tremendous amount to be gained by simply staying with the more demanding conversations that occur in our immediate surround-ings. Establishing personal connections with those who are different from us is immensely valuable. These connections serve to reduce our ethno-centrism and tendency to "otherize" fellow humans, and they support the development of deep, positive regard.

There are several stories about anti-gay Republican members of Con-gress who changed their views on homosexuality because one of their family members came out. Because of their relationship with them, the legislators' private views on sexuality changed, even if their public posi-tion didn't. They didn't want to deny the truth of their loved ones' expe-rience, nor did they want to risk damaging their personal relationships.[8] Growing through conflict means that we learn how to stay open to new information and perspectives on the issues that we feel passionate about. To do that, we have to stay committed to the conversation, and to the well-being of ourselves and others.

There may be issues where we don't change our position, but by stay-ing in the conversation we change our way of talking about it, and we change our relationship to the other side. Several years ago in Boston, following the fatal shootings of abortion providers by pro-life extremists, a dialogue initiative was developed by the Public Conversations Project (now known as Essential Partners).[9] Its purpose was to bring key mem-bers of the two opposing sides to the table to talk. Through mediated civil dialogues held in secret over the course of six years, people had the opportunity to clarify a common language, express themselves openly, deepen their grasp of the conflict, and understand that the other side was not going to go away.[10] The only option was for each side to get to know each other and find a way to extend mutual respect. In the end, the pro-lifers and pro-choicers remained committed to their respective positions.

However, they began demonstrating ways in which their relationship had changed. The groups defended each other in the press when inflamed rhetoric rose up from time to time. They both moderated tensions and showed support for each other. A religious leader on one side of the divide publicly discouraged another leader from his own church from visiting his parish because he knew that the visiting leader tended to speak aggressively about the other group, and he didn't want to expose his parishioners to that. Through this humanizing process, regard deepened between the two groups; the public discourse changed, and the violence eventually diminished.

There is a lesson here for public dialogues that can be applied to the online world. With important conversations proliferating over the internet, the various subcultures risk falling into patterns of segregation. Online forums draw together like-minded people and usually reject challenges to their account of the truth. There are many valid concerns about the lack of healthy dialogue in the online world. It's a hard thing to balance. On one hand, it's extremely important that social media gives marginalized groups a platform on which they can share their experiences, cultivate solidarity, and build community. It is legitimate to create safe spaces and protect against aggression from trolls, including stalking, death threats, and physical violence.

On the other hand, closed-off groups risk becoming echo chambers where people confirm one another's views and ideologies. Conflict can erupt within these subcultures and can quickly turn toxic, leading to blocked accounts and the "cancel culture," the current trend of exiling people online for making problematic remarks, without attempting to communicate directly, resolve the conflict, or employ due process.[11]

We need to host more humanizing conversations online to counter the intense polarization that has emerged. In online communications it is important to remember that we lose a tremendous amount of information when we translate our intentions and thoughts into words, captions, sound bites, emoticons, and GIFs. If we mean to have conversations that matter to us online, we would be wise to practice emotional and social maturity. This means taking responsibility for our reactions, pausing to reflect, slowing down, listening carefully, and always leaving room in our mind for the possibility that we may have misunderstood the message.

We should remember to take a moment to think about who we're talking to—the real human being on the other side of the communication—and ask ourselves what we actually know about them. Furthermore, what is our intention, and how does it connect with theirs? We can ask what a positive outcome might look like. If engaging with someone feels out of integrity with our standards for a relationship, we should gracefully withdraw from the conversation and redirect our energy. If it's a conversation that matters to us, we might find ways to improve the quality of the connection, such as moving from texting to the phone, from an audio connection to video contact, from an asynchronous to a synchronous interaction in real time. Then we can do our best to work with some ground rules.

Despite our human struggles, Diane is convinced that we are in fact moving toward greater goodness, truth, and beauty.[12] Taking the long view of history and seeing the revolutionary positive changes we have undergone can be immensely encouraging. As a human species we have made enormous gains in the last two hundred years, to grow through conflict and overcome previously insurmountable differences.[13] Seeing conflict as a developmental opportunity supports us as we learn to accommodate more diversity in our personal relationships than ever before. We can learn to see our discomfort and mistakes not as barriers to our growth but as a necessary part of our emergence, both individually and collectively.

THE PRACTICE

1. Think about your last conflict.
2. What identity was most activated in you? For example, were you a parent, a partner, an employer, a friend?
3. Is there another identity that could have had a role in that conflict?
4. How would the conflict have changed if you had shifted to a different identity?

15 *Shadow in Conversation*

> Between the idea
> And the reality
> Between the motion
> And the act
> Falls the Shadow.
>
> —T.S. Eliot, "The Hollow Men"

Every conversation is made up of a combination of what "I" think and feel, and what "you" think and feel. "I" refers to our sense of self, to our thinking, feeling, embodiment, and will. Sometimes we think of "I" as the ego. Freud used the word *ego* to represent the mainstream of the psyche, that is, the ordinary part of our self-concept that mediates between our primitive instincts, the id, and the urges of the superego. The superego demands better from us, often criticizing and challenging our self-concept to be more and better, while the ego is the ordinary voice that helps us navigate the commonplace events of our life, managing everyday ups and downs and mediating between the primitive id and the superego.

Another way to think about the ego is that it maintains homeostasis in the body-mind. In biology, homeostasis refers to stability within a cell or a body. Just as the cell keeps a balanced internal environment by adjusting to conditions and resisting change, so the ego adjusts constantly to affronts and challenges to it, recalibrating often in order to stay as close as possible to a set point. The ego creates an equilibrium in our self-image and lends stability to how we see ourselves.

Viewed through this lens, we can see the ego not merely as a psychological structure or as an impediment to spiritual development, but as a mechanism by which the self maintains its identity, using as little energy as possible and returning quickly to a state of equilibrium and familiarity. This perspective applies not just to our individual ego but to our collective self-identity. Members of groups constantly push away information that challenges the stability of their group identity, and like the individual, they maintain their self-concept within a familiar range.

But to grow up, mature, and change, the ego must be disrupted. It must expand to include more positive versions of the self, and at the same time it must accommodate aspects of the self that it would rather not consider. A mature ego is one that can balance positive inputs with realistic assessments of its own shortcomings or weaknesses. It is open to feedback from others and gives up idealized notions of the self as well as extreme versions of inadequacy or lack of self-worth. In this process of maturation, we no longer experience our self as fixed or solid but as flexing and flowing according to situations and conditions. Paradoxically, one develops more confidence in oneself and, at the same time, is deeply humbled by the lessons of ego development.

What Is Shadow?

One of the greatest disruptors of the equilibrium of the ego is the shadow. In Jungian psychology, *shadow* refers to aspects of the personality that remain out of the light of awareness because we find them unacceptable, shameful, or dark, the opposite of how we like to think of ourself.[1] In Ken Wilber's usage, the word *shadow* is any part of our self that we cannot hold in our first person "I" and is usually projected onto others who are not like "me."

How does shadow occur? These disowned parts once belonged fully to our experience. Little kids have no problem being thoroughly themselves. But through social conditioning and other life pressures, some aspects of our self pose a threat to our self-image. They are too painful, too shameful, or simply too unacceptable to contain. So to maintain equilibrium in the self-sense, the unacceptable shadow material is pushed out of awareness and instead is projected onto others. For example, "I'm not angry, you are," or in groups, "We're not racist, they are."

But of course, shadow traits continue to function in the background, causing confusion, distress, and difficulty for our self and others. You can see them at work in the moral crusader who has illicit sex on the weekends, or in the politician who while campaigning against corruption is busy taking bribes. But we can all catch glimpses of different shadows in ourselves, if we dare to look closely enough.

An example of shadow came up in a conversation recently between some young longtime friends of Gabe's. One of their group showed up on social media wearing a Palestinian scarf, a keffiyeh, the oversized black-and-white checkered scarf that Yasser Arafat made famous, which symbolizes Palestinian solidarity.[2] This was complicated by the fact that he was an American Jew who felt strong political support for the Palestinians. Some members of the group were also Jewish and viewed it as anti-Israel and therefore anti-Semitic. Others protested that it was a form of cultural appropriation[3] and felt critical of their friend for wearing it since he was not Arab.

A heated conversation among the friends broke out at a gathering one night shortly after the photo appeared, when the scarf-wearing friend wasn't there. Most everyone held strong negative opinions about him wearing the scarf, but they disagreed about what to do. Some were inclined to reprimand him directly, while several felt more interested in hearing his perspective. They thought that because he was a friend, he should be given the benefit of the doubt. Maybe he had a rationale worth listening to. At least, they argued, he should be engaged in conversation so they could all understand more fully his motives for wearing it. And as his friends, they could directly share with him the negative perceptions they had about it.

But the majority of the group was not so conciliatory. They rejected any support for him as a betrayal of their shared values. They were firm that he should already know better, and because he had misfired on social media he should feel direct heat from them in response. They also said that speaking out on his behalf automatically supported cultural appropriation, anti-Semitism, or possibly even terrorism.

Soon the small subset of supporters was overwhelmed by the intensity of the others, and they fell silent. The topic soon changed, and the group never brought it up again, with the friend or with one another.

Shadow in Conversation

There are, of course, different ways to interpret this event. One could view it simply as an example of friends testing group norms. Another perspective might be to see the social cost of political stands, since relationships often suffer when people take a position. Or the rift may have erupted from the inability of the group to hold the tension of multiple perspectives in conversation, and so the majority simply dominated the smaller group right out of it. There is likely some truth in all of these perspectives.

We can also use this story to look at how shadow works. As we said before, shadow exists where a trait or characteristic cannot be experienced as "I," "me," or "us." In this instance, the man wearing the keffiyeh was identified by the group of friends as "other." In that moment he represented the oppressor, while they saw themselves as protectors—protecting Israelis or Jews from hostility, or protecting Palestinian or Arab culture from appropriation. They were operating on behalf of actual or perceived victims, and the scarf-wearer was *not* one of them.

When some friends spoke up for him, they were perceived as the oppressor's ally, and therefore they fell into his camp. Next, the protectors became the oppressors themselves. They quashed free speech and open dialogue and imposed their perspective as the only legitimate way to see things. Of course, this group of friends probably couldn't see the irony, but that's the effect of shadow: We can't see it. We can't see how, when we attempt to protect, we can oppress. Or how, when we stand for tolerance, we become intolerant. Or when we promote understanding, we fail to understand.[4]

It's important to acknowledge that there are real victims of oppression in the world, and it is right for fair-minded people to call out transgressions and apply pressure for social change. Social change happens in the broad strokes of black and white, for and against. But in the territory of interpersonal conversation it is notable how often people identify as victims or protectors, and not as oppressors. It is very rare indeed for someone to consciously own the role of the oppressor and acknowledge the ways that they have lorded it over others. Remember that our ego's job is to maintain its identity, so it makes sense that the part of us that has hurt others remains in shadow, outside the light of awareness.

Owning Shadow

In many conversations, because the role of the oppressor is largely rejected and foisted onto others, the conversations themselves will sometimes bear the weight of this shadow in the background. It is as though the oppressor is lurking about in the room. The dialogues can feel tremendously heavy, with an overweening sense of injustice and wrongdoing. There is little room to make mistakes or inhabit nuances, shades of gray, or paradoxes because there are certain dogmas that must be adhered to. Some conversations that purport to be open are not at all open because there is almost no room for differing opinions.

Understanding how shadow plays out in conversation can be extremely relieving, especially in discussions where people want to exchange perspectives and learn from one another. In the context of this kind of group discussion, shadow work could be introduced by simply asking everyone in the conversation if they would be willing to take a few minutes and identify ways in which they have oppressed or injured others. The inquiry can include anything from dominating a younger sibling, to breaking a lover's heart, to maligning someone at work, to causing a car accident, to participating in an unjust social system. Engaging our shadow is the simple willingness to identify with the qualities or actions that we ordinarily assign to others unlike us.

This question usually disrupts the way we commonly think of ourselves. And when people have the ego maturity to engage shadow work, it is tremendously energizing. The whole room combusts into enlivened explorations, where villains are no longer outside the room but are right here and now, living among us. And it *is* everybody, all of us! Suddenly, the foreboding sense of shame and blame gives way to the recognition that everyone is, to some degree, complicit in creating human suffering, and is therefore capable of helping to relieve it.

When shadow work becomes a regular part of how we engage conversation, the boundaries of individual ego and the group identity become a lot more flexible. People are able to take responsibility for incidents of injury and for the legacy of injustice. It is easier to see the ways that "I am angry" or "we are being racist." Remember: to grow up, the ego must be disrupted, so we must learn to include aspects of our self-identity that we would rather not consider.

Shadow is like the oil of the psyche. It is dark, heavy, and unprocessed, but when it is accessed, it releases tremendous energy. Self-identity expands to include more experiences; energy begins to flow, and compassion naturally arises. People will often laugh or cry. Heaviness in the heart gives way to a lightness of being. Sometimes new insights emerge, or new creative strategies and actions result. Because everyone is on board, we can travel together in sharing responsibility for our human predicament. After doing shadow work, we have witnessed men and women talk about how they have hurt one another. People of color have listened patiently while white participants want to take responsibility for racism. One trans woman compassionately told the room to be easy on themselves when relating with her. "It's awkward," she said, "to get the pronouns right, even as I'm trying to get them right myself." It's very touching when self-responsibility and care blooms naturally in an environment of curiosity and awareness.

Conversation is great practice in this regard because there is always an opportunity to see unwanted parts of our self in the other. Imagine the conversation between the friends who engaged in the scarf discussion if they had taken a moment to do some shadow work. They could have identified with the victim in themselves, with both the fierce and determined protector and, most importantly, with their own oppressor. What if they had thought about a time or place when each of *them* had been the person in the photo wearing the wrong thing for the wrong reason? Would it have changed their perspective? Would the outcome have been different? Shadow work doesn't change the situation, but what it does do is change the way we relate to the situation. It almost always opens up more possibilities for insightful, compassionate, creative responses.

Golden Shadow

Usually, shadow refers to invisible aspects of the self or the group that are largely negative. There are also, however, positive aspects of identity that may remain hidden from our awareness. This is called the *golden shadow*. The golden shadow creates the same kind of challenges to the ego, by disrupting homeostasis. You may notice how sometimes we resist accepting our positive attributes or shy away from receiving praise. Compliments can sometimes offend our notions of who we are, creating a defensive response in the body and cognitive dissonance in the mind. But as we said earlier, a maturing ego expands to consciously include more positive versions of the self as well.

Bringing out the golden shadow might involve taking time to acknowledge the upside of our suffering. Diane may decide to share how mothering a child with a cognitive disability, while challenging, has deepened her respect for difference and reorganized her idea of intelligence. Gabe might acknowledge the deep bond that black folks share, as well as the cultural riches borne directly from oppression, like gospel singing and the blues. This is not to deny the pain or devastating exploitation that is the story of black people in America. But resilience,

strength, and creativity are another part of that story that sometimes remains in shadow in conversation.

We cannot grow or change without disturbing the boundaries of the
ego or without expanding how we tell our stories. When we disrupt them,
there is an opportunity to reshape our identity. As we move into more
open space, relaxing and letting go rather than contracting and holding
on, a new possibility for exchange arises. By taking back our projections
and including unacceptable parts of our self and of others, we create a
sense of inner integrity, mercy, and wholeness in our own mind and in
conversation with others. We develop more flexibility in our identity. We
cease to judge others so harshly, and take more responsibility in our ongoing struggle for fair, loving relationships.

THE PRACTICE

The 3-2-1 of shadow is a practice developed by Ken Wilber, with Diane,
at the Integral Institute.[5] Choose a quality in a person that disturbs you.
You may feel critical or annoyed by it. Then follow the three steps of the
process:

Step 1: Face It

Using a journal, describe the negative quality of the person in vivid detail using the pronouns *he/him, she/her, they/them/it*, and so forth. This is
your opportunity to vent. In doing so, explore your experience fully, particularly what it is that bothers you. Don't minimize anything. Take the
opportunity to describe the disturbance as fully as possible, and what is
wrong with it.

Step 2: Talk to It

Now enter into a dialogue in your journal, and talk directly with this quality as though it is a character using the pronouns *you/yours*. For example,
if you are working with anger as the shadow quality, address the anger as
though it were a being. This is your opportunity to make a relationship
with the shadow. You may ask questions such as "Who are you? Where

do you come from? What do you want from me? What do you need to tell me? What gift are you bringing me?" Then allow the disturbing quality to respond to you. Allow yourself to be surprised by what emerges in the dialogue.

Step 3: Be It

Now, writing or speaking using the pronoun "I," become the person with this negative quality, and write about what it's like to be you using *I/me/ mine*. See the world entirely from the perspective of the one inhabiting this quality. Describe what it's like to be you. What do you see? Why are you here? What's right about you?

16 *Miraculously Resilient*

Character cannot be developed in ease and quiet. Only through experience of trial and suffering can the soul be strengthened, ambition inspired, and success achieved.

—Helen Keller

Kim's sister has worked with many queer artists from Asia and the Middle East, helping them bring their work to conferences and film festivals in London. She was particularly moved by one young Syrian artist, Alqumit Alhamad, who shared his story with her.[1] His life changed dramatically when the Islamic State in Syria and Iraq (ISIL) invaded and took power in his hometown of Raqqa, Syria. Alqumit is a gay man in his early twenties who had been studying art at the University of Aleppo, and ISIL's extreme stance on homosexuality became a real threat to his personal safety and that of his family. Having no other choice, he said devastating goodbyes to his family, and at great risk journeyed to seek refuge in Europe.

Making his way from Syria to Turkey, he took an inflatable boat across the Aegean Sea to Greece. The boat, which was only supposed to hold twenty people, had sixty onboard. Of the three boats that left that day from Turkey, only his boat arrived safely to shore. One boat sank, and what happened to the other one is unknown. Making it to dry land, however, was only the beginning of another chapter in his harrowing journey.

After moving through multiple countries over several exhausting and uncertain months, he finally settled in Sweden, where he now lives with a host Swedish family. Seeking to create the best life for himself and his loved ones, he is now working to bring his brother from Syria to join him. But he still experiences the deep pain of being forced to leave his family and homeland behind. Alqumit harbors anger about the circumstances that forced him to leave his country: the ISIL invasion, the subsequent limits to his freedom, and the dangerous prejudice against homosexuality in Islamic extremism. His artwork is often therapeutic, and through it he faces his own personal traumas and the collective grievances of his people. He also delves into other crucial issues for refugees, immigrants, and LGBTQ people. He is, in his heart, a powerful activist, intimately shaped by some of the most challenging hardships one can endure in a lifetime.

Innate Resilience

It is sobering to listen to the story of Alqumit's life, his ordeals and that fateful boat trip as a refugee. Yet his will to live is powerful, and his art expresses a provocative inquiry that is both raw and courageous. In hearing stories like Alqumit's and contemplating his work, we have to ask how it is that human beings find the strength to live after suffering traumatizing and life-threatening experiences. What can we learn about people's abilities not only to cope and recover but to develop true resilience?

Resilience, as defined by the American Psychological Association, is the process of adapting well in the face of adversity, trauma, tragedy, threats, or significant sources of risk.[2] Severe trauma can include suffering serious physical and psychological harms like the loss of a loved one, homelessness, war, or other damaging consequences of economic, natural, and political turmoil.[3] In stories like Alqumit's, building resilience means fortifying one's ability to endure those traumas, integrating them into one's psyche, and releasing the body and mind from the grip of the experience.

Building resilience and adaptability is a natural capacity of all forms of life. But people are not equally resilient. Resilient people are those who bounce back, who grow, adapt, and improve their ability to handle injury and threats to their well-being and survival. Resilient societies are ones that can evolve to creatively deal with threats to their stability and balance. For example, the term *resilience* is frequently used to denote a country or region's ability to cope with climate change and increasingly volatile natural disasters.

Disturbances in the System

Our understanding of the psychological and physiological effects of trauma on people has deepened enormously in recent years. We have developed a scientific understanding of how trauma continues to live in the body,[4] creating ripples throughout the nervous system,[5] leaving imprints in the neural pathways and conditioning our way of reacting to the world.[6] Trauma keeps us in the past. We remain stuck or reactive rather than supple. When we have experienced trauma and the experience remains unintegrated, the initial emotional and embodied responses are held in the body and mind, and we continue to react as we did originally. As one student who studies trauma told us, "Trauma is not what happens to you; it's what stays with you."

People who are traumatized are often caught in the bodily sensations, memories, and responses to past experiences, unable to access fresh or new options that might be available as actual events unfold. Cognition also becomes stuck or repetitive. One typical stuck point involves personalization, the belief that you are to blame for every problem; another is pervasiveness, the fear that an event will affect all areas of your life rather than just one; and a third is permanence, the certainty that your feelings or your situation will last forever.[7]

Bessel van der Kolk, an expert on trauma and embodiment, says that the big issue for traumatized people is that they no longer own themselves: a loud sound, a random comment, or an unexpected change can hijack their attention, flooding them with stress hormones, cutting off access to their thinking and rendering them helpless to control or manage their response.[8] This can look like shutting down or withdrawal; sudden, unexpected outbursts of anger; expressions of hopelessness, shame, or self-recrimination; or outright panic. People lose their ability to think clearly, to speak, or to make sense of what is happening. From the outside, these traumatic responses may appear irrational and disproportionate, like a simple inability to cope, but from the inside the intense response feels completely appropriate, legitimate, and real.

Trauma and Conversation

When Diane worked for the courts in Utah, she helped develop a victim-offender mediation program in the juvenile courts. These programs were part of a larger restorative-justice movement aimed at bringing additional depth, value, and humanity to the traditional judicial system. Victim-offender mediation programs facilitate victims meeting with their offenders and discussing the circumstances surrounding the crimes. The mediation allows victims to discuss the impact of the crime on their lives and gives offenders an opportunity to express themselves, including whether they feel regret or want to take responsibility. The victim can participate in the sentencing phase of judicial proceedings and make creative recommendations to the court regarding restitution.

At the time, victim-offender mediation in the juvenile court usually involved less serious crimes like vandalism, theft, and other misdemeanors. One day Diane received a call from the adult criminal court. It was a judge who had an unusual request of her: He was involved in the sentencing of a man charged with assault with a deadly weapon. A woman had been stabbed in the arm at a party, and her attacker had pled guilty to the crime. As part of the sentencing, the victim had asked the judge if she could meet with her attacker, since he was someone she knew, and she felt it would help her healing to be able to talk to him about what had happened.

Today, victim-offender mediation programs that address violent crimes are more common.[9] But at the time this was a completely new idea for Diane, and she had lots of doubts and questions. Was it safe? Would the victim be retraumatized by simply meeting in the same room with her attacker? Was the assailant capable of a productive conversation? Was he accountable for what had happened? Remorseful? The list of questions was long. Diane took a few days to do some research and some thinking. Then she responded to the judge, saying that she was open to the idea but suggested that a mediation would require some preliminary assessment and preparation.

She met several times with the woman and her therapist. The woman was certain the conversation would be helpful to her. Her therapist was also supportive. Diane explained the process, and together they came up with a list of important issues and questions that the woman wanted to talk about, including the events that led up to the attack, the assailant's state of mind, and so on.

Diane also met with the offender and prison personnel. She wanted to ensure that the man understood that the meeting was not designed to lighten his sentence, but to give the victim a chance to participate in the judicial process. She encouraged him to engage truthfully and to say what he needed to say. He seemed to understand the purpose of the meeting and consented to it. Although it wasn't a condition of the conversation, he said he wanted to express his remorse.

Diane remembers very little of what was said between the two people the day of the mediation but what she does recall is the intensity of the felt experience. She remembers everyone at the table together and an overwhelming sense of fear. She couldn't tell exactly whose fear it was; it seemed to pervade the entire room. She remembers the trembling in the voice of the woman as she spoke, her labored breathing, and a rash that appeared on her neck and chest. Diane heard her speak rapidly and urgently in bursts, imploring the man to explain why he had attacked her. At times the woman paused and cried for a few minutes. At one point she sobbed. She told the man how hurt she was, physically and emotionally. She said she was confused by the assault, as they had been friends. She said how surprised and frightened she had been when he attacked her.

The man said very little during their hour and a half together. Mostly, he listened quietly to her with his head down, nodding. He told her he couldn't explain it. "It happened so fast," he said. "I was drunk." And "I was angry." And "I am so, so sorry." The woman seemed to be able to hear him, and gradually she relaxed. Her speech slowed and her voice softened. Her mind seemed to finally settle and rest in the present.

The meeting came to its conclusion. In the end, there wasn't anything surprisingly insightful about their conversation. There wasn't a remarkably poignant moment of understanding that flowed between them or a tearful scene of forgiveness. But there was a willingness to sit down, to ask questions, and to talk to each other. It meant that they had to remember vividly what had happened, and most importantly, they had to relive the intensity of the experience, and feel it completely in an effort to heal. In the end, they made human contact. That was all.

When trauma is alive in conversation it has certain common characteristics. There is often emotional and physical intensity, a feeling of dread or danger, and tremendous uncertainty. There is always a feeling that we probably should not talk about this. Unprocessed trauma can erupt in personal conversations, and it can come up in groups. Diane has felt the potency of its presence in conversations between English and Afrikaans speakers in South Africa, between Israelis and Palestinians in Tel Aviv, and in conversations between people of color and white people in the United States. Lisa Hartwick, a friend and fellow Zen practitioner who lives and works with indigenous people in British Columbia, Canada, is always intimately aware of the legacy of adversity and pain that First Nations people have endured. Sometimes trauma is acute, like in the incident involving the woman and her attacker in the mediation session, or a story about a police stop. Sometimes, however, it is prolonged, collective, or intergenerational. But having conversations that turn toward unprocessed material, even when it involves trauma, builds resilience.

When recognizing the signs of trauma in conversation, we should always proceed with caution, making sure that we have the skills to handle it. (And if we don't, we can suggest supportive resources). We should ask permission before talking further and demonstrate more presence and patience than usual. It helps to be able to soothe oneself and others by remembering to go slowly, by directing awareness to the here and now, by giving reminders that we are for each other, and while the subject matter may be painful, to observe that the current situation is safe. We may take simple steps to help recalibrate our nervous system, like breathing deeply and intentionally together, or taking a few minutes to sit in silence and just feel, or by connecting with the elements—the earth, the wind, or sunlight.

By making space for the discomfort and distress rather than treating it as a barrier to connection, we have an opportunity to practice being present, trusting our humanness and allowing awareness itself to support our healing. These intentions align with currents of nature that, when supported, show how amazing the life force is. It is a sign of health to want to include and integrate what's hard, uncomfortable, or deeply painful into a wider and deeper spectrum of our experience. Skillful conversation is itself a practice of building resilience and suggesting resources for people when the process is out of our scope.[10]

Reconciliation and Resilience

Sometimes, talking about traumatic experiences is one of the few options we have. In Rwanda, the Association Modeste et Innocent is a nonprofit organization that supports long-term national efforts toward reconciliation twenty years after a horrible genocide ravaged the country wherein nearly a million people were killed in a matter of months.[11] The people who actually did the killing and the survivors are led through a series of preparatory processes, culminating in the perpetrators' formal requests for forgiveness for the harms they have caused. These harms include awful incidents of the murder, rape, or torture of loved ones, the burning of homes, or the destruction of property and possessions.

Sometimes there are very practical reasons for reconciliation. Making peace might be essential for people to simply survive. In developing countries, people struggling on a subsistence standard of living may have little choice but to stay in relationship with the other people from their village, regardless of their history together. Reconciliation in these cases can mean that a widow will still be supported for the rest of her life, or a child will be provided for while she grows up. Still, it requires incredible emotional strength and courage to engage in conversation and to pardon the people who have committed these terrible acts of violence.

One Rwandan survivor says, "I used to hate him. When he came to my house and knelt down before me and asked for forgiveness, I was moved by his sincerity. Now, if I cry for help, he comes to rescue me. When I face any issue, I call him."

Another says, "I realized that I would never get back the beloved ones I have lost. I could not live a lonely life—I wondered if I was ill, who was going to stay by my bedside, and if I was in trouble and cried for help, who was going to rescue me? I preferred to grant pardon."

A third woman speaks implicitly to resilience when she remarks, "If I am not stubborn, life moves forward.[12]

Within these communities, the formal process of reconciliation literally brings neighbors back into relationship, reweaving the local social fabric and fortifying their shared resilience. Like Alqumit Alhamad, the people in Rwanda startle us out of our conventional notions of the permanent nature of harm, inspiring us to reflect on the human heart's capacity to recover, to genuinely forgive, and to stay in relationship, even after experiences of extreme trauma.

Whole and Complete

Examples of reconciliation and resilience remind us how, through the greatest misfortunes or heartbreaks of life, a part of our self longs to recover and to remain in relationship. As we open to the more difficult parts of our life, we may also open the more painful parts of our self. The more intimate we become with our own bodily sensations and the spectrum of our emotions—the madness, anguish, and awkwardness—the more capable we are of being present to those same difficulties in others.

All human beings share a profound desire to experience happiness. We are never alone in that sense. Similarly, our experience of suffering is shared. We may not have endured the same kind of injury or the same degree of pain, but each of us has been subjected to threat and has experienced harm.

Remember, however, that trauma keeps us in the past. So it is important to know when in conversation we are processing trauma that is alive, felt, and real, ready to be acknowledged and integrated, and to distinguish it from a preoccupation with talking about our wounding. We can notice the difference because the very vital signs of trauma are replaced by rigidity, repetition, a deadening of the life force, or a heaviness that feels anything but wakeful. It is possible to become stuck in that habit of old wounds and to fail to notice all that is new, fresh, enlivening, and free in this very moment. If we are not stubborn, life moves forward.

Every conversation about trauma or abuse would be well served if it included an acknowledgment of the miracle of our resilience and the remarkable capacity for redemption in the human experience. We are fully capable of facing our pain, integrating it more deeply into our psyche, and even though it would have never seemed possible, letting go of the grip that it has on our attention. And like Alqumit, we are tremendously creative and resourceful in the face of the grave difficulty of our suffering.

THE PRACTICE

Tonglen is a heart-based Tibetan Buddhist practice that anyone can do. It teaches us how to feel our pain and transmute it into great compassion.[13]

1. Open space: Bring your awareness to your awakened heart, the ultimate part of your being that is present, clear, and boundlessly open.
2. Feeling: As you breathe, become intimate with your sensations. Breathing in, take in any qualities that are dark, heavy, or uncomfortable. Breathing out, send out light, coolness, spaciousness. Notice a bias or familiarity toward the inhaling of darkness or the exhaling of light. As you breathe, practice equanimity, realizing that both are a part of our experience.

3. Self: Bring to mind your own suffering. When you inhale, breathe in any feelings of shame, disappointment, frustration, insufficiency, or overwhelm you might be feeling. When you exhale, breathe out tenderness, self-love, or empathy—anything that opens up your heart to a sense of universal expansion.

4. Others: Next, breathe in the pain of a specific person—a friend, parent, or animal you wish to help. Breathe out loving-kindness or spaciousness to that person, or send the gesture of offering someone a good meal or a safe bed for the night. Notice again if you have a bias, whether it is easier to do the practice for yourself or for others. Let curiosity guide you as you continue cultivating an attitude of impartiality toward both.

5. Universal: Extend the wish to relieve suffering from a specific person or being to all beings who share that experience of suffering. In this way you can use particular instances of suffering as a stepping stone to the universal suffering of all beings everywhere. On each cycle of breath, bring in all pain, loss, or contraction, metabolizing it in the space of emptiness and alchemy, and release great love, spaciousness, and images of what would be healing to all.

17 *To Atone and Forgive*

We must develop and maintain the capacity to forgive.
He who is devoid of the power to forgive is devoid of the
power to love.

—Martin Luther King Jr., *Strength to Love*

Gabe's first job out of college was as a first-grade teacher. He remembers seeing two of his first-graders, Scott and Andrew, best buddies, sitting together on the steps during snack break, sipping from their juice boxes, talking about the newest apps on their parents' phones. They were completely connected, and Gabe said it was a delight to watch them as they took turns listening and talking excitedly to each other.

Then Andrew fell silent in midsentence as his attention became totally absorbed in the small bag of Cheetos he had pulled from his lunch box. He unselfconsciously began licking his lips as he went to open the bag. In the same instant, Scott eyed the snack, and something primitive in him took over. His body slowly and deliberately shifted into the posture of a predator ready to pounce. And the moment Andrew opened the bag, Scott struck. He swiped the bag out of Andrew's hand and shoved his hand into it first, grabbing a fistful of Cheetos for himself. The carefree flow of conversation instantly turned into a shocking brawl filled with screams, fists, and tears.

Gabe pulled them apart, and once the emotions cooled he asked Scott, "Why did you do that?" With a face contorted with confusion and disbelief, he said weakly, "I don't know . . . I just wanted some chips." His confusion was real to Gabe, who could see from his vantage point that Scott had been taken over by a primitive instinct that cut off all the connection, care, and mutual regard he had for his friend just seconds before.

Self-interest works like that. It narrows our attention, constricts our open awareness, and disconnects us from the larger web of relationships. In the process, we inevitably hurt one another. If we are honest, we can see that our egocentric impulses and ethnocentric habits assert themselves constantly, creating disruption, tension, and conflict in our relationships. It's easy to feel cynical, succumbing to the simplistic conclusion that as human beings we are instinctive, aggressive, and totally at the mercy of self-interest, creating divisions and consequently more suffering for ourselves and others.

While true to some degree, this limited view fails to acknowledge our inherent capacity to grow emotionally, relationally, and spiritually.[1] This capacity for growth was entirely apparent in Gabe's first-graders. Over the school year they grew like weeds, not only physically but also in their ability to self-regulate, empathize, and extend care and concern to their peers. And when, like Andrew and Scott, they caused injury to their classmates, they learned how to make up for their mistakes by apologizing, forgiving, and moving on.

We are fallible beings. We make mistakes in judgment all the time. Psychologist and economist Daniel Kahneman describes in his book *Thinking Fast and Slow* the shortcuts that our brains take in order to make sense of an incredibly complex and confusing world, a process that results in errors. Realizing that we make frequent mistakes is a source of humility and compassion.

All the great spiritual traditions emphasize practices of reparation for dealing with our mistakes. Christianity, the religion of Gabe's late grandmother, emphasizes forgiveness, and Zen, the spiritual practice he engages in, stresses the importance of atonement. These function like two wings of a bird. Atonement gives us an opportunity to make amends when we have done harm, and forgiveness frees us from bondage when we have been hurt. Both are deeply powerful acts that help us reestablish our connections with one another when relations have been disrupted. Atonement and forgiveness release us from the cycles of revenge, bitterness, and victimhood. Learning to atone and forgive supports our growth because no matter the injury, trauma, or injustice, we can always find ways to reconcile and transform ourselves and our relationships for the better.

Like Scott and Andrew, who quickly made up, it is important that we learn how to use these skills with people we're close to. But atonement and forgiveness may also be viewed from the perspective of culture, and we can see how on a large scale they have been used to help an entire people move forward.

Truth and Reconciliation

South Africa endured forty-six years of institutionalized racial segregation, from 1948 through 1994. Apartheid is a system that overtly discriminates against nonwhites. The South African government operated as a police state that violently oppressed any dissidence against the regime, and many black South Africans were murdered or disappeared for their resistance. When the apartheid regime came to an end, South Africa elected Nelson Mandela as their new president. He was an antiapartheid leader who believed that white and black South Africans could reconcile and heal the divisions caused by apartheid. He said, "No one is born hating another person because of the color of his skin, or his background, or his religion. People must learn to hate, and if they can learn to hate, they can be taught to love, for love comes more naturally to the human heart than its opposite."[2]

One of Mandela's first initiatives as president was to establish the Truth and Reconciliation Commission (TRC), whose task was to provide support and reparations to victims and their families and to compile a full and objective record of the effects of apartheid on South African society.

The commission hearings were for the benefit of the victims of injury and trauma, and their testimony helped to inform government reparation efforts.[3] But the hearings were also for the benefit of the operatives who had worked for the repressive regime. Amnesty was offered to them if they were honest about their involvement, confessing their actions and revealing how the system had operated. The TRC had the practices of atonement and forgiveness woven into the commission's process. Archbishop Desmond Tutu, a Nobel Peace Prize recipient and chairman of the TRC, was asked by a reporter what he hoped the world would learn from the TRC, and he said, "I wish for everyone to know that any situation can be transfigured."[4]

What Is Atonement?

There is a simple definition of atonement that derives from the Zen tradition: to reflect on one's misdeeds, confess them to an individual or community, and repair the negative consequences of them.[5] To be truly accountable for our mistakes we need to be aware of the context of our misdeeds and clarify or reconnect to the ethical principle, community standard, or vow we hold ourselves to.

As you know, in the work that we do as facilitators, one of our essential ground rules is to be for each other. This means that we are committed to recognizing our bonds with one another, even when differences or negative experiences arise. When we deviate from this agreement and create separation, hurt, or misunderstanding, we atone by confessing or expressing the mistake, repairing the relationship, and realigning our minds and behavior with this ground rule. Our shared goal is to create a culture in which we freely give and receive constructive feedback that allows us to grow our self-awareness, take responsibility for our habits and their impact, and refine our conduct. When this ground rule is observed, nobody is viewed as fundamentally bad or wrong; instead, we are helping one another become more conscious human beings. From a Zen perspective, the practice of atonement teaches us to reflect on our actions and bring them into greater harmony with all our relations and the world.

Why don't we atone more easily or more often? Why do we often deny wrongdoing when we know we have had a negative impact? Or why do we not come forward and take responsibility when we know we have caused injury? The short answer is that the ego protects itself. We cultivate an image of ourselves that is "good," and admitting our shortcomings threatens this delicate self-image. Confessing our mistakes to ourself is difficult, but sharing them with others is even riskier because we lose control of how others will perceive us. We fear damaging the relationship, being punished, or becoming alienated.[6] But when we're willing to confront our mistakes, we make a deeper connection with ourself and with others. It's quite a relief to drop the narrow self-image of always being a "good" person.

What Is Forgiveness?

Desmond Tutu defined forgiveness as the act of abandoning our right to resentment and revenge, and opening to those who have harmed us in order to make a new beginning together.[7] It is a commitment to relate to others' humanity, understanding that we are each fallible, yet we have the ability to change, grow, and transform our way of being. Most importantly, we forgive in order to release our hearts and minds from the trap of resentment and hatred.

We can extend our compassion by seeing others' negative actions in the larger context of their life circumstances and karma. Errors do not happen in the vacuum of a single personality; they arise from a complex set of causes and conditions that contribute to the injurious behavior. It is through this larger lens that a new beginning can be imagined by both parties. This does not mean ignoring the misdeed, injury, or injustice that has been committed, but it does mean that we choose not to allow it to be a barrier to our relationship in the present.[8]

We often resist forgiving in the same way we resist atoning. We're afraid that forgiveness will backfire and leave us vulnerable to further harm or abuse. Sometimes we're simply not ready, and sometimes the prospect of forgiving disturbs our self-image—we're fearful of becoming a pushover or a doormat.[9] But research confirms the positive benefits of forgiveness, including lowering blood pressure, decreasing depression, and healing psycho-emotional trauma,[10] so we should seriously consider including forgiveness in our life. Even though it can be challenging, we can, through conscious engagement, learn to forgive and atone.

Growth through Atonement and Forgiveness

The three of us led a workshop in Oakland, California, that focused on race relations. It was attended by a diverse group of people ranging from spiritual seekers from Marin County, to students from UC Berkeley and Stanford, to community organizers from San Francisco and Oakland, and some people from tech companies working in human development. The group dynamics reflected the racial traumas of the past and was emblematic of the racial tension of the present moment in the United States. Even though everyone agreed to the ground rule to be for each other, participants were fundamentally aligned and loyal to their own group and racial identities. We found ourselves mired in divisions, alienated from one another, with no clear way forward or out. These divisions deepened after the following exchange between a participant of color and a white participant:

"I think white liberals are more dangerous than the KKK," exclaimed a black participant. Confusion, unease, and a sharp anxiety rippled through the space. Diane observed the room. "Who here identifies themselves as a white liberal?" she asked. All the hands in the white group went up, some more tentatively than others. "So this comment refers to you," she said, "not to someone in the abstract. How do you understand it, and how do you feel about it?"

"How can you say white liberals are more dangerous than the KKK, that doesn't even make sense," protested a white participant. "The KKK is racist and deliberately violent."

"Because," said another African American participant, "at least we

know where a KKK member stands in relation to us. We can protect ourselves because we know exactly how they're going to behave. But with
white liberals, some of you here from Marin County, we can never really
know."

There was a clear division in the conversation as reflected in a palpable tension in the room and defensive speech by white and black participants. This deep division was impacting Gabe as a facilitator. He tells the
story this way:

Diane pulled him aside and gave him feedback: "You seem to be losing your neutrality as a facilitator, Gabe. What I mean by that is that you
are advocating for one group, rather than encouraging everyone to listen
to one another."

"I am?" he said with surprise and curiosity.

Gabe could see some truth in what Diane was saying. He could feel
his frustration toward the white participants mounting and a striking
absence of frustration toward the people of color. He felt that the white
participants deflected or made excuses not to deal with the history of prejudice and bigotry, while his fellow brothers and sisters of color couldn't
make that same choice. If he was honest, he believed that the white participants could offer more, do more, and say more than they were. In this
he strongly identified with the people of color in the room and felt alienated from the white people there, and this identification was contributing
to the sense of separation in the room. What was happening?

As he looked more closely at himself, Gabe could see that his anxiety
about being biracial, specifically the old accusation that he was "not black
enough," was surfacing, compromising his neutrality as a facilitator. He
felt reluctant to support the white participants because if he did, he feared
he would be seen as selling out his people and regarded as weak in their
eyes. He could see that in this he shared the same dilemma as others: they
were all finding it difficult to be loyal to their group, and at the same time,
to stay open and available to those from the other group. It was a tight-
rope walk.

To work with this impasse, participants broke up into caucuses, one for people of color and one for white people. The goal of each group was to address this double bind between loyalty to one's own kind and commitment to building bridges and creating a worldcentric conversation. How could each group take responsibility for the stuckness in the dynamic and support the whole group in moving forward together?

Forgiveness and Love

As the people of color explored the issue in their caucus, they discovered the reason for their resistance to the white participants was due to the fact that they really weren't ready to receive apologies or offer forgiveness. Being available in any way felt like a betrayal to their group's long history of suffering. Mark Reko Fabionar, a participant of color and an elder in the workshop, recognized this dilemma and reminded everyone of the words of Martin Luther King Jr., who said, "Within the best of us, there is some evil, and within the worst of us, there is some good." [11] Which is to say, people of color are not purely good, and white people are not purely bad. Mark invited them to close their eyes and visualize their ancestors standing behind them.

"Now," he said, "all cultures, communities, and lineages have their gifts as well as their limitations and shadows. This is a natural part of being human. In this workshop we want to practice collectively naming and releasing some of those limitations and challenges of our own lineages, even if only for the day or a moment, so that we can have more spaciousness to connect with our white brothers and sisters."

They were then invited to feel into the limitations of their lineage, limitations that, as Mark said, were likely defensive patterns that served a survival function in the past or present. In this ritual they created an opportunity to let go of those limitations and open up to new possibilities. Mark invited each one in the group to speak out loud, stating something that they were willing to release in service of new possibilities. Each participant of color took a turn using the following sentence stem: "Today I release . . ." They then completed the sentence with responses like "my distrust of white people," "the mindset of being a victim," "misplaced and destructive anger in my lineage," "my suspicion of white women," and so on.

Finally, Mark invited them to present the gifts they might use to bridge their differences with the white participants in order to create greater understanding and connection with them. Each person took a turn, starting with the words "Today I give . . ." Some of their statements included: "the message that my ancestors would be overjoyed if we came together today," "compassion," "love and forgiveness," "a space for white people to be heard."

Atonement and Self-Responsibility

Diane, who facilitated the white caucus, now tells the story from her perspective:

When they separated into smaller groups, the people in the white group didn't want to belong to that group at all. They were alienated from the process, and from one another. They also had a dilemma: They wanted to be accountable for the suffering that has been propagated by racism in the United States and be responsive to the people of color in the room. At the same time, they resisted the feeling that they were inherently bad and wrong for being white. Many felt hopeless about being able to establish a meaningful connection with the people of color, since their previous efforts at communicating had failed. Some wanted to continue and try to connect, while others were more despondent, doubting that it was possible.

They started by doing some shadow work, picking up on the accusation that as white liberals they were not fully committed to change. Diane asked them to identify with the part of themselves that really didn't want to make a change. They each took turns: "I don't want to face pain." "I don't want to give up my privileges." "I don't want to be blamed for the past." "I like being in power and I don't want to give it away." "I feel hopeless." "I don't really care that much." The shadow work seemed to clear the air.

Then she posed the question, "What would it take for you to want to be a member of this group? Who would we have to be so that you would want to belong?" They engaged this question with some genuine curiosity and came up with these ideas: They wanted to participate fully and be accountable for the oppression of the past and the racism that is still alive today. They wanted to do this without conditions, without an agenda for how the people of color would respond. They wanted to communicate and offer an apology of some kind and let it stand on its own terms, regardless of the response. On all of this, they agreed. Their cohesion as a group was then established. One member, Dave, asked the white caucus if he could take a risk and share an "accountability poem" with the participants of color. The white caucus gave him their support.

Eventually, the two groups came back together. Gabe remembers feeling a tremendous amount of goodwill pervading the whole room. A quiet, respectful silence opened up between everyone. The work the groups had done in the caucuses was having an enormously positive impact.

Dave asked if he could speak directly to one of the women of color, Rachel, who was a natural leader in the workshop. She accepted, and he read his poem, which spoke to the legacy of slavery and how white people had contributed to that legacy. He spoke about his commitment to grow in awareness of his own racism and to work to create more equity in his sphere of influence.

Rachel listened carefully, attentively, along with the rest of her group. When Dave was finished reading, Rachel quietly thanked him, along with other members of the group. Then one of the men of color, someone who had been quite passionate earlier, said, "I've been groomed to be a warrior for my people. For the first time in my life I feel like I can put down my sword." The accountability poem was a form of atonement, the listening and receiving an opening for forgiveness. To atone and forgive are practices to remember that we are all one. As Martin Luther King Jr. said, "Forgiveness is not an occasional act; it is a permanent attitude."[12]

THE PRACTICE
Practicing Forgiveness

1. Partner with a friend who can be a nonjudgmental listener as you explore forgiveness for a harm committed against you. Remember that forgiveness does not mean reconciliation necessarily, but is an opportunity for you to release into openness and a sense of well-being.
2. Describe the situation and the person who harmed you and the impact on you. In your description, be specific about what was hurtful.
3. Ask your partner to reflect back to you what they heard. What is it like to hear someone repeat the story back to you?
4. Now explore with your partner how you would like to forgive this situation or person. Reflect on the fact that forgiveness is to free yourself from any suffering you may still be feeling.
5. Identify whether there is an action that you would like to take to symbolize your forgiveness. It could be simple, like burning incense or writing a letter of forgiveness.

Practicing Atonement

1. Partner with a friend who can be a nonjudgmental listener as you atone for a harm you have committed against someone else.
2. Describe the situation, the behavior, or the action you committed that created harm and the effect it had on the person you harmed.
3. Ask your partner to reflect back to you what they heard. Notice the impact of hearing your story repeated by someone else.
4. Explore with your partner whether there is an action that you would like to take to symbolize your atonement. It could be simple, like bowing or writing a letter of apology.

18 *Becoming Wholehearted*

There is no battle between good and evil, positive and negative; there is only the care given by the big brother to the little brother.

—Thich Nhat Hanh, *True Love*

Our work is to help people talk about our differences so that we can learn to appreciate, negotiate, and integrate them. When we don't, we can't, or we won't, they become deeper and much more dangerous. As we can see today, our differences can grow to pervade our politics to such a degree that ordinary conversation becomes strained or impossible. Daily news broadcasts become so polarized that we don't get the news, we get a sustained dose of us-versus-them, contributing to our collective stress and feelings of unease. Our differences can intensify into full-blown conflicts, where violence breaks out, where political demonstrations easily become deadly, and where random shootings occur regularly. And meanwhile we find ourselves involved in ongoing military interventions, wars, and conflicts around the world that are immensely costly to the environment and the social order, not to mention destructive to human life.

Human life is fraught with uncertainty, loss, and inherent pain. But in times when the cultural atmosphere is negatively charged, energizing our differences and expanding the divisions between us, we must take a strong stand for our own wholeness and engage in practices that develop the full capacity of the human heart. Love, compassion, patience, and equanimity soften the harsh realities of the world. They transform our smallest differences into understanding and our greatest divisions into harmony and peace. This idea may seem sentimental or idealistic, but spiritual traditions have always taught that the greatest asset we have in life is the human heart. The heart can reconcile what the mind cannot; it can metabolize our pain, transform our grief, dispel our impulse toward violence, and integrate all that appears unacceptable to us into the seamless whole of life.[1]

Surrendering to the Heart

At one point in Kim's life, finding a connection to her own heart provided her with the respite she badly needed in a troubling world. After graduating from a university environment she had truly loved, she was living alone in London in the throes of post-breakup blues. She was struggling with the demands of law school and managing too many volunteer roles in an attempt to feel like she was making a difference. On top of that, she was obsessed with learning about human rights, which confronted her with the global reach of injustice and suffering, something she thought would become the focus of her law career.

This combination gave her a head full of constant worry. She was distressed about those people who were being persecuted and disappearing at the hands of brutal governments. She was uneasy with her fellow law students, especially when they made fun of her politics, and occasionally, her ethics. She was disquieted by her feelings of loneliness and worried whether she would be able to find a group of true friends, people she could trust and talk to honestly about how she was feeling. At times she would lie awake, feeling hopeless and alone, her mind racing with all these questions and anxieties.

One night, lying awake in the dark, overcome with exhaustion and frustrated at her inability to relax and simply fall asleep, she decided she had to do something. So she stretched her arms wide open, palms up in a gesture of surrender. She closed her eyes and silently asked for help, not knowing who from. As she listened, silent and completely fatigued, she sank into her physical being. She noticed the heaviness of her body, each limb completely supported by the bed and her head sinking into the pillow. She felt the gentle weight of the blanket on top of her and the warmth that surrounded her. Seduced by these calming sensations, her mind slowed down. Sinking deeper into her body, she visualized her awareness moving out of her head, through her neck, throat, and shoulders, into her chest. Then she heard her heartbeat. She listened quietly, and for the first time Kim became intimate with the sound of her own heart beating. She felt a sense of immense relaxation and was able to completely accept who and where she was in that moment of her life. She drifted off into a deep sleep, her mind and body resting in a state of peace.

Kim repeated this practice every night and turned to it whenever she had trouble with destructive mental patterns. As the seasons changed, she began to feel more balanced and capable again. She has never forgotten what she learned that night. Meditating on her heart offered what her mind could not: a way of reconciling the conflicts within herself and accepting her own struggles.

Vietnamese Zen teacher Thich Nhat Hanh reminds us to be grateful for our pain and suffering, as they are necessary for us to understand the wholeness of our experience.[2] In other words, to create space for our suffering and struggles is to become wholehearted. It is vital for us to learn from the painful moments of life so that we can gather the energy of compassion, love, and understanding in this present moment and use its momentum to carry us forward.[3]

The Heart's Intelligence

The heart is located at the vital intersection between the brain and the gut in the body's anatomy. It is the engine of our circulatory system and is central to our emotional regulation. On a subtle level, it is the fourth of seven major chakras,[4] and its role is to integrate the denser, more instinctive part of our earthly experience with higher cognition and spiritual illumination. It is noteworthy that in the West we often define mind and heart as being distinct. Ancient Chinese sages, however, believed that the heart was actually the center of human cognition.[5] In Chinese, the word *xin* translates as both "heart" and "mind," but depending on the context it can also mean "core," "intention," or "emotion."

Equanimity is another capacity of the heart. It includes the beauty of our human experience and our suffering. It anticipates the ups and downs of life, the ins and outs, and allows for them both. Our thinking mind is usually binary, highlighting opposites such as black or white, and intolerant of ambiguity or shades of gray. Our life is full of contradictions that create difficulties for the mind. But the heart's intelligence tells us that even though there is injury, injustice, and oppression, our life is fundamentally worthy. Working with these difficult challenges provides the conditions that allow us to develop the heart's innate intelligence and its ability to hold paradoxes and contradictions in a way that the mind cannot.

The heart's most powerful asset is its ability to love, which means to open to the beautiful part of our human experience as well as to that which is painful, and include them both. It is a powerful symbol of our deepest values, and it represents our interconnectedness. It provides us with the ability to extend openness and care to all beings, regardless of any flaws, errors, or harms of the past. The poet bell hooks questioned people about what force in their lives had compelled them to make a profound transformation, from a will to dominate to a will to be compassionate. They all reported that the transformation occurred as a result of experiences grounded in love.[6] Thus it is love that provides the most transformative power when it comes to addressing our ills and catalyzing our movements against oppression and toward justice and fairness.

Doc Childre, founder and CEO of HeartMath, describes heart intelligence as "the flow of awareness, understanding and intuitive guidance we experience when the mind and emotions are brought into coherent alignment with the heart. This intelligence steps down the power of love from universal source into our life's interactions in practical, approachable ways which inform us of a straighter path to our fulfillment."[7]

Cultivation of heart intelligence is absolutely essential to being a whole human being. We live in a world where birth and death come hand in hand, where loss is an inescapable reality, where suffering ranges from the commonplace to the horrific, and where justice is an aspiration that must always be demanded and fought for. Our spiritual awakening depends on a willingness to acknowledge these challenging realities.

His Holiness the Dalai Lama refers to the "spirit of emergence," where only after understanding how utterly vulnerable to suffering we are can we become sufficiently disillusioned with our negative habits of mind and with the behaviors that create so much of our suffering.[8] This disillusionment has a calming effect on the mind and opens us up to our deep, unconditioned nature. This is the subtle part of ourselves that remains undisturbed by the ups and downs of life. By coming to terms with our predisposition to suffer, we can access tremendous compassion for ourselves and others.

Thinking back to that difficult period in Kim's life, by meditating on her heartbeat and relaxing with her life exactly as it was, she demonstrated the heart's innate ability to transform troubling experiences into a deep sense of self-acceptance. The practice opened up a calming sensation of respite and softened the resistance she had to her mental anxieties. It helped to reduce her fear of her feelings, and when she became less afraid she was better able to see clearly and act with confidence in her life circumstances.

Compassion

The emotional domain is the gateway to the heart. In other words, working with our feeling states, both positive and negative, contributes to the development of emotional maturity and to the heart's intelligence.

Each of us has learned to deal with our feelings differently based on our upbringing, culture, and developmental stage. Some of us suppress or avoid feelings; others seemingly drown in them, while still others dramatize and act them out in all kinds of unhelpful ways. Whatever the nature of your habitual emotional patterns, there is always an opportunity to practice and refine the ways you experience and process emotions. This involves being willing to feel your emotional state, while at the same time letting go of those feelings when they no longer serve you.

Releasing negative emotions that have become solidified in the psyche is necessary to one's well-being. As one saying goes, "Holding on to anger is like drinking poison and expecting the other person to die."[9] Anger, like other intense emotions, is not wrong, but there's a point when it's worn out its usefulness, when it's no longer a source of clarity, or boundaries, or personal power, but is simply a grudge held in the body and mind. And when this is the case, we need to let it go.

Cultivating positive feeling states is perhaps even more important. Studies on compassion and empathy by neuroscientist Tania Singer and colleagues at the Max Planck Institute show that compassion training increases positive feelings and activates the corresponding brain networks associated with positive emotions.[10] Other research in the field of social and developmental psychology confirms that people who feel compassion in a given situation help others more often.[11]

Three positive feelings that are supportive in our relationship with others and that can make a difference in our conversations are sympathy, empathy, and compassion. The dictionary treats these three as synonyms, but there are nuances in meaning that are important to developing our skills in conversation. It turns out that there is research that shows that there are actually distinctive differences in our brain activity,[12] especially between feeling empathy and feeling compassion.

Sympathy is feeling sorrow or pity for another person's pain. The *Merriam-Webster* online dictionary describes it as "an affinity, association, or relationship between persons or things wherein whatever affects one similarly affects the other." For example, if a friend's father has passed away or if we encounter a destitute person, we can cognitively relate to their suffering and feel for it, but we can also maintain some emotional distance.[13] It is clear that their grief or misfortune is not ours.

Empathy involves more intimacy and emotional exchange. When we empathize, we feel the pain or suffering of others and recognize the felt experience of that suffering in our self. Rather than "feeling for," we "feel with." It's akin to relating to the suffering of a close friend or family member rather than to a stranger's. Scientists explain that it is through the activation of mirror neurons that we experience empathy. These are brain cells that respond to witnessing someone else having an experience as though we are having that same experience ourself.[14] This is the reason why many people in the helping professions experience burnout—they are literally registering others' pain and suffering that same experience in their own bodies on a daily basis. This can lead to social withdrawal and negative health outcomes.

Compassion, on the other hand, also feels the pain of others, but unlike empathy, there is no distress signal in the brain. Because of this difference, compassion can actually preserve and reinforce the calmness of the mind.[15] And in this way, compassion is a renewable resource.[16] Furthermore, we can train in generating compassion, thus relieving the burnout that results from empathy alone.

Compassionate activity is energizing and contributes to the transformation of many difficult situations, even the most intractable conflicts. We have many collective challenges facing us today, and while these problems can feel overwhelming to us, as Thich Nhat Hanh says, "If love and compassion are in our hearts, every thought, word, and deed can bring about a miracle."[17] Our current challenges present a golden opportunity to expand our hearts and strengthen our compassion. Because of the available energy of compassion, it increases our courage for acting in the world rather than withdrawing and becoming depressed, despondent, or cynical.

Courage

Martin Luther King Jr. is an exemplar of compassion's power to provoke the courage to confront injustice despite overwhelming odds. King's last speech, delivered the day before he was assassinated, is a wholehearted expression of this compassion-fueled courage:

We've got some difficult days ahead. But it doesn't really matter with me now, because I've been to the mountaintop. And I don't mind. Like anybody, I would like to live a long life. Longevity has its place. But I'm not concerned about that now. I just want to do God's will.

And He's allowed me to go up to the mountain. And I've looked over. And I've seen the promised land. I may not get there with you. But I want you to know tonight that we, as a people, will get to the promised land.[18]

In reading the words of this last speech of King's, there is the distinct impression that he was in two places at once when he spoke. He was, of course, in front of the congregation he was speaking to. At the same time he seemed to be speaking from the "promised land," a place in the heart where "little black boys and black girls will be able to join hands with little white boys and white girls as sisters and brothers," a place where justice, freedom, and peace reign.[19] Perhaps his courage was born from a sense of what the compassionate heart is capable of. When we glimpse the worlds that are possible by enacting our compassion, we become more emboldened and courageous to transform our current conditions.

THE PRACTICE

1. Put your hand on your heart region and breathe as if you are breathing to and from the heart.
2. Allow the breath to come and go while opening to whatever sense of well-being is present in the heart region.
3. Then notice if there is a disturbance in your field, a question or an issue that needs resolution.
4. Next, allow your heart to hear the question, to receive it.
5. As you continue to breathe and to feel, listen to your heart and receive any response from the heart to your question. Just relax, feel, and listen.

19 *Freedom Here and Now*

Do not forget the luminous nature of your own mind.
Trust it. It is home.

—*The Tibetan Book of the Dead*

Kim sought out meditation and spirituality because she had deep, unresolved questions about impermanence and suffering. From a very young age she remembers thinking about how humans and all other forms of life, from tiny ants to great blue whales, feel pain, struggle, and ultimately, die. Spiritual teachings help us come to terms with this stark reality by acknowledging that impermanence and suffering are a part of life. Sitting still in meditation, observing body, breath, and mind, we learn to be present to all experiences as they arise. Whether sadness, joy, loss, or gain, it is all included in the open, unbiased space of awareness.

A moment of profound acceptance came to Kim as she sat beside a river in Singapore, listening to a talk a friend had shared. It was a recording of Diane facilitating a process called *Evolving Worldviews.*[1] Diane invited the audience to explore and share as they looked through the lens of the four different stages of human development: egocentric, ethnocentric, worldcentric, and Kosmocentric. Each stage represents a shift in identity, with its own distinct values, insights, imperatives, hopes, and fears.

Kim listened to the talk on her MP3 player as participants described their experiences of these nested identities. They articulated small, familiar egocentrisms, full of desires and dreams, and how in this state they were overcome with fear and stress, doing the lonely job of simply surviving. Audience members then described their experience relating to the ethnocentric stage of development, notable for its love of group identity, protection in numbers, and belonging, and decorated with the values of duty, obedience, and self-sacrifice. But it was also apparent from participants' comments that this stage of development, with its concrete thinking, black-and-white beliefs, and a dangerous inability to accommodate difference, is inflexible. An ethnocentric self is easily threatened by others. In that state we divide the world into *us* and *them*, and make *them* our enemies.

When the audience members identified with the worldcentric self, they felt more expansive, freed of the limits and constraints of their local groups, open to adventure and distinctions of all kinds, including various beliefs, values, and worldviews. They expressed a natural curiosity about others and an openness to different perspectives. They discovered their identification with all of humanity and with the planet and her many, varied life forms. On the downside, they also described the overwhelming scale of problems around the world: the refugee crisis, the arms trade, sex trafficking, the plague of illicit drugs and the violence that surrounds them, and the profound loss of plant and animal life. They empathized with people and suffering beings everywhere.

Kim felt these descriptions strongly resonated with her own experiences. She had spent a lot of her childhood moving between Asia and the West, and she could see how the us-versus-them mentality of ethnocentrism gave way to greater belonging and connection when shifting to a worldcentric point of view. But she also could see the reach and depth of global problems, and how solutions would require cooperation at a scale unlike the world has ever seen before. She had often felt engulfed by the troubles she saw. At times, the issues seemed impossibly overwhelming.

It was difficult for her to overcome a sense of despair and find hope for the future.

As Kim sat on the bank of the river listening to the broadcast and re-calling her own worldcentric challenges, she heard Diane asking if par-ticipants were ready to expand their perspective yet again. Diane then asked them to speak with the voice of the Kosmocentric self. Despite static in her headphones and the background noise of people talking as they walked down the nearby path, Kim sensed an immediate change in the atmosphere of the group in the recording. When the audience identi-fied with the Kosmocentric self, there was a sudden feeling of calm, peace, and restful presence.

Responding to Diane's gentle questioning, Kim heard people describe their experiences. They conveyed a sense of spaciousness and an immedi-ate awareness of the here and now, free of any preoccupation with the past and the future. They recognized their unconditioned awareness, not di-vided by notions of good or bad, better or worse. They saw ordinary pref-erences lose their significance, and they expressed an ability to see things clearly, as they are. They experienced the innate beauty of reality, and yes, there was pain, but the suffering was no longer so searing. Compassion is a natural response to life's dilemmas, and by shifting into compassion they were free of the anxiety that something was terribly wrong. Kim re-members being so powerfully moved by this that it brought her to tears. It was a moment of opening, of touching a greater awareness and seeing the possibility of a new way of being in the world.

We seek to evolve conversation so that we can move fluidly between our ego identification, our ethnocentric loyalties, our worldcentric cares, and the freedom and calm that a Kosmocentric perspective brings us. We learn to relax in our profound sameness, explore our vivid and ex-ceptional differences, and become confident in the durability of our rela-tionships. We practice flexibility in our perspective, loosening the grip of calcified stories and ideas about who we and *those people* are. We listen more honestly and clearly, without clouding the message with hidden bi-ases and past impressions.

"A hundred years is nothing in the eyes of an Afghan," Kim once heard someone say—a reference to a cultural stereotype of the Afghan people and their supposed appetite for revenge. A hundred years is nothing to any of us when our blind spots go unnoticed or unchallenged, and our patterns persist. Through compassionate conversations, we can challenge our views, learn to tolerate discomfort, and be glad when our eyes open and divisions dissolve. We begin to trust our perennial desire for connection and understanding, and are amazed by our innate instinct toward growth. We just need to practice our skills—seriously practice them—and relate to people in a way that brings our deepest values out into the open.

The Role of Spirituality

The great spiritual traditions have, throughout history, been a resource for seekers of truth, healing, and reconciliation. The world's religions have created coherent systems of values, ethics, and social codes, framed around recognition of a higher power, a greater awareness, and elevated ways of being. They have developed practices to support these values such as prayer and meditation. They have written texts with tremendous depth and beauty that include powerful descriptions of a vision of human life. And they have enacted this potential in their ritual forms and community gatherings. The same religious traditions have also wounded us, disappointed us, and betrayed our trust, but in a process of evolution, the wounding, disappointments, and betrayals play a part in refining and revitalizing these remarkable systems of human transformation.

So what is the role of spiritual insight and practice when it comes to our subject, having compassionate conversations? For some, spirituality and religion have no role to play at all. For them, bias and injustice are features of the very concrete, hardscrabble reality of a material world, and nothing other than that belongs in the conversation. For them, enlightenment occurs when rationality prevails over faith, when reason tops emotion, and when practicality holds sway. From this perspective, spirituality is viewed with suspicion, doubt, or even contempt. Karl Marx's words still ring true for many secular materialists: "Religion is the opium of the people."[2] For materialists, religious people need to go into rehab.

Yet peace groups very often have been faith-based. Mennonites, Quakers, Baha'i, and Jews have all been committed to conflict resolution and transformation work throughout their individual histories. We have recently seen how in the West the Zen Peacemakers order was established by Bernie Glassman; and Ten Directions, founded by Diane and Rebecca Ejo Colwell, who are both informed by Integral Theory and Zen study and practice, is training facilitators and grounding them in meditation.

The black churches in America, with their uplifting preaching and transcendent gospel singing, have offered incredible spiritual sustenance and social support of all kinds, providing for the poor, establishing schools, and attending to the needs of prisoners. They have been central in maintaining social cohesion within the black community, so it is natural that many leaders in the civil rights movement came from there. Zen teacher Merle Kodo Boyd describes how black religion has sustained people in circumstances that were nearly impossible to survive, let alone flourish or raise a family in. She says that the black church "came into being organically in order to help slaves endure slavery, and that sense of endurance is still needed."[3]

For all these people, then, there is no social justice conversation without a spiritual foundation. As one of Gabe's friends, Kelsey Moss, says, "Sometimes it's because of our suffering that we seek spirituality." And Diane says, "In discovering spirituality, we seek to alleviate suffering." The essential themes of forgiveness, atonement, union, and enlightenment are forged in our religious traditions, and the great traditions can still be a source of deep guidance, inspiration, and comfort in the meaningful conversations of our times.

Then and Now

Part of what makes conversations about social justice difficult is our tendency to look backward through the lens of history. When Kim was doing her postgraduate studies she remembers one of her professors emphasizing the importance of grasping the history of a conflict in order to better understand what's happening today. He argued that we have to account for the depth of people's memories of conflict in order to fully transform the present situation. He suggested that peace interventions based on a shallow or incorrect understanding of the past are poorly designed and will not last. In fact, they can make things worse.[4] One common theme in the struggles of many oppressed people around the world is that their grievances, wounding, and the negative impact of racist or sexist history on their lives has never been fully recognized or addressed with authenticity and care by those in power. So hearing people's stories and legitimizing them is essential to transforming conflict.

The past has profound implications and must be reckoned with. But like we often do in our personal relationships, we look backward far more than we do forward. And even more problematic, we overlook what is occurring in the present.[5] And it is right here, right now, that we can find the potential for change. We can acknowledge what we know of the past, but to change a pattern of any kind requires our full attention in this moment. Now is when old biases prevent us from listening. Now is when privilege obscures clear seeing. Now is the moment when anger alienates potential allies. Now is the time when strategies are designed and action is taken to change things in the present. How do we want to live now? How can our ideals be realized in the present circumstances, with these very same people? The past is long gone, and the future has not arrived. But the seeds of a different future are always planted in this very moment, through the choices we make and the behaviors we enact *now*.

Many times we resist recognizing the freedom and potential of this moment. In our personal lives and in our collective memory, the suffering and struggles of the past have such a grip on the mind that relinquishing them, even for a few minutes, is disorienting. We fear that we'll feel groundless, unprincipled, cowardly, or traitorous, that we're betraying ourselves or our culture and ancestors. We may wonder how we can avail ourselves of conversation and connection in this moment when the people we are conversing with are our relative's historical enemies. That is the awesome challenge we face.

Yet it is the only way people have ever moved forward. Healing and transformation don't demand that we forget our history, not at all. But they do require that we change our relationship to pain and overcome our attachment to injury. People can often accomplish this on an individual basis, but in conversations between groups, the pressure of ethnocentrism is intense. As we said before, our desire for loyalty and our fear of betrayal may prevent us from making real contact in the here and now. Kelsey, who is a scholar of race and religion, shared her experience of what it is like as a black woman to loosen her loyalty to her ethnocentric identity to explore the freedom she truly wants:

> I could stay in a committed relationship to the affirmative, expansive, and creative aspects of blackness, of my black identity. At times I could release the pain, trauma, and resistance that was so often deeply bound up in that identity. As much as I wanted to retain that ethnocentric consciousness and feel connected to this community of color, both those who surrounded me in that moment and my lineage, I realized that the ultimate thing that communities of color had struggled for and dreamed of was freedom.[6]

For us, cultivating mindfulness and awareness in dialogue opens the domain of true freedom. Zen teacher Norman Fischer says, "Learning to let thinking come and go, we can eventually understand a thought as a thought and a word as a word, and with this understanding we can find a measure of freedom from thoughts and words."[7] The same is true of our stories and history. Identifying with them for a purpose and then letting them go, we can see that they are stories and history and nothing more, and we can find a measure of freedom from them and not be bound by them.

Worthy of Compassion

When asked what his greatest fear was, His Holiness the Dalai Lama responded that he was most afraid of losing his compassion for the Chinese. Even after decades of persecution of the Tibetan people by Chinese authorities, he remains convinced that the Chinese are worthy of his compassion.[8] He could have been cynical, bitter, despondent, or even hateful, but the depth of his spiritual practice shines through. He shows us how practice orients us to the better part of our nature, refreshes us when we are tired and disillusioned, and nurtures virtues like patience, forgiveness, and compassion.

For us, there is a place for spiritual insights and practice in these conversations. A spiritual approach can help us bring more humility, patience, and generosity into our engagements. It can include the significance of the past as well as a vision for a more equitable future, all the while encouraging us to be fully in the present. Some might say that to relinquish one's attachment to identity is a capitulation. But from another perspective, tasting the freedom that is always available to us when we loosen our grip on identity is a spiritual gift that keeps us refreshed, revitalized, and present in this very moment.

THE PRACTICE

1. Think about a belief you held in childhood that you no longer believe to be true.
2. Think of a time as an adult when someone else moved you to seriously reconsider one of your strong ethical or spiritual beliefs.

How did these instances of shifting beliefs impact your sense of freedom and possibility?

20   *In It Together*

Do not be daunted by the insurmountability of the world's grief. Do justly, now. Love mercy, now. Walk humbly, now. You are not obligated to complete the work, but neither are you free to abandon it.

—attributed to the Talmud

A friend and colleague of ours, Julian Gonzalez, is an engineer helping the City of Vancouver mitigate the damage of rising sea levels. Rising seas and storm surges are already impacting farmers, residents, and businesses along the Pacific Coast of Canada. Julian and his team are helping to design and implement planning that will assist Vancouver in adapting to the effects of climate change over the next hundred years. While the solutions could be fairly straightforward, implementation is difficult because of strained relationships and conflicting interests among stakeholders.

Julian believes that climate change won't be the end of humanity. The real threat is what people pose to one another when they are frightened, stressed, and overcome by aggressive and primal tendencies. Under stress we regress,[1] becoming highly self-protective and less altruistic, and prone to violence. We defend ourselves and our own group at the expense of others. But people who are self-realized, capable of regulating their nervous systems and managing their fears, can think clearly and act compassionately even under enormous pressure. These are the ones best suited to help *all* of us through the climate crisis and whatever existential challenges we face in the centuries to come.

Facing these challenges will require our commitment and practice. Every time we practice with intention we shift from being passive players to active participants in our own evolution. You could say this is our evolutionary opportunity. Of course, the changes we seek will take time; in fact, they will take well beyond our present lifetime. That is why an evolutionary perspective is so important—it helps us take a very long view on our vision, allowing us to cultivate patience and trust in the moment and in the enterprise of life itself. Using the Integral framework to address transformation provides us with the following four important ways we can practice to bring about our vision of the world.

Enhance Our Awareness

As they say, all change begins with yourself. Our ability to become mindful, aware, and present has been shown to be essential in the fostering of our personal as well as our collective well-being.[2] Our personal interior, while perhaps invisible to others, is very apparent to ourselves—that is, if we choose to look.

Awareness can be expanded, and attention can also be narrowed, like the lens of a camera, so that we can watch and witness the workings of our own individual sense perceptions, thoughts, feelings, and defensive patterns, as well as our beliefs, values, and intentions. Meditation practice is tremendously supportive when it comes to cultivating awareness. By sitting in meditation, we can gain a greater ability for self-observation, seeing the workings of our innermost reality more honestly and clearly. By sitting in meditation, we can learn to accommodate our experiences, whether positive or negative, and we can reduce our tendency to react and judge ourselves. Everything quiets down in the space of being fully present, where one's essential being shines through. This is what Ken Wilber calls "waking up."

There are additional ways we can cultivate the interior dimension: intention-setting; psychotherapeutic work, educating oneself in philosophy, history, and social change movements; and integrating the insights of adult developmental psychology. These methods support meditation practice in facilitating awareness. In this way we can become familiar with how we self-identify and observe the connection between our ideas about our identity and how they play out in the world.

Transformation of our inner experience allows us to shift our sense of who we are, from a fixed, unchanging personality, to a person who can grow and change. Expanding our sense of self allows us to expand our circle of care and concern. There is an aphorism, "If you change the way you look at things, the things you look at change."[3] If we want to live in a more compassionate world then we must tend the soil of our inner lives and water the seeds of compassion within us. To make this personal choice is to take a giant step toward freedom.

Evolve Our Skills

Any skill, from playing the piano to negotiating peace treaties, requires engagement, repetition, a willingness to make mistakes, and engaging again. We must listen, ask questions, express our thoughts and feelings clearly and directly, and pose challenges. In our work these are important interpersonal skills involved in good communication. The more we practice these skills, the more they become available to us when conversations become tense and emotionally charged. Old habits of reactivity are replaced by new habits of inquiry and open-mindedness. Developing our skills makes for better working relationships—and better relationships form the basis of clear, efficient activity.

For example, the business world, which typically focuses on goal setting, efficiency, action, and profit, is increasingly turning its attention toward the "soft" skills of interpersonal work.[4] And yet one of the most common complaints of American workers is poor communication within an organization. People often report that poor communication and dysfunctional interpersonal dynamics prevent them from doing their best work. So learning these interpersonal skills can have tangible benefits for businesses.

But practice isn't easy, and we don't always want to do it. Just recently, Willie ran into his sixth-grade teacher, Deb, at the gym. She wanted to say hi to him, but he was annoyed because he was lifting weights and didn't want to be interrupted. So he complained about this to Diane, saying that he had had a "falling out" with Deb at the gym and didn't want to talk to her anymore.

Diane said to him, "Willie, what do you mean you had a falling out with Deb? She probably just wanted to say hello to you. Just take a few minutes and say hello to her."

"Don't tell me what to do, Diane," he said. "I'm not like you. I'm a Utah Devil [a sports team he plays for in his imagination], and I am not one of your people."

Damn, Willie. Spoken in the true spirit of us versus them.

Even if he were "one of her people," Diane can't get Willie to do anything he doesn't want to do. That's true for all of us—we can't make people do what they don't want to do. But conversation is one of the few universal human activities that is known to bring people together. And we can make significant contributions in this direction when we have the right skills.

Engage Our Culture

This aspect of practice involves belonging to a group, tribe, or culture. It deals with the space between us, including our values, principles, and shared meaning-making. One Zen master says that our practice is our life.[5] So our practice must always include other people. Practicing together is ongoing, continuous, and full of repetition and surprise.

Conversation is inherently a practice that can build and potentially transform culture. It can have immense power to help us explore what is possible, clarify what matters to us, deepen our relationships, and cast a light on our shared reality. Dialogue is the cornerstone of all significant changes to society and to our efforts to create fair and equitable conditions for everyone. And it is itself a manifestation of our ability to create the kind of reality we want to live in, treating other people in the way that we ourselves want to be treated.

We watched a movie recently that illustrates this point. *The Dawn Wall* follows the journey of rock climbers Tommy Caldwell and Kevin Jorgeson. After six years of meticulous preparation, they made their way up an impossibly sheer rock face called the Dawn Wall, in Yosemite National Park, California. The movie shows their remarkable ascent against the backdrop of a vast and stunning natural landscape, as they take turns belaying each other up the many pitches of the wall. Each man provides support for the other, while a whole crew of people back them up from below, sending up groceries, water, lip balm, sunglasses, and encouragement.[6]

The movie culminates in the question of what really matters when Kevin is unable to successfully traverse a difficult pitch halfway up the wall, and Tommy begins to go it alone. Kevin abandons his personal goal of success and gives all his energy to supporting Tommy in making the ascent. But just as Tommy is about to arrive at the top, he suddenly feels that a solo accomplishment is empty of meaning. He has a profoundly beautiful moment of coming to this truth when he decides to suspend his finish and throw all of his energy into supporting his partner, Kevin, in getting over his stuck point. He does so happily now, joyfully, and who knows, maybe because of the extra determination to do it together, Kevin finally succeeds. They climb to the top of the wall as one very triumphant team.

It is such an inspiring moment, and it is an illustration of the bodhisattva vow of Mahayana Buddhism. The bodhisattva makes a vow not to cross over to the state of complete enlightenment until all beings have crossed over. This is the power of a shared vision, mutual effort, and the full recognition of our interdependence. As Chögyam Trungpa Rinpoche has said, "Those who take the bodhisattva vow make one simple commitment: to put others first, holding nothing back."[7]

An evolving culture is one in which people have committed to be for each other. It's a simple choice to keep company with people who inspire and strengthen us, and do the same for them. Our groups may enact a full range of values and spiritual virtues: from loyalty, duty, and self-sacrifice; to hard work, high performance, and efficiency; to inclusion, diversity, and equity. We want to be in conversation with people who hold a range of value sets, and we especially want to reflect our blind spots to one another, deal with our power relationships, give and receive feedback, and see ourselves in the flex and flow of evolution and change.

To make the most impact, we need to practice in a community. As John Lewis, a civil rights giant and US congressman, is fond of saying, "A beloved community is possible."[8] It is a community that is united and diverse, one that acts with wisdom and compassion, relates in ways that do not divide, and creates greater liberation, fairness, and collaboration. These are communities that long to be in harmony with others and with the planet.

Transform Our Systems and Institutions

It is sometimes said that anyone who says they are not interested in politics is like a drowning man who insists he is not interested in water. We might add that anyone not interested in the functioning of their institutions is like a starving woman who insists she is not interested in food. Public education; the justice system; public health networks; financial institutions; the worldwide system of agriculture, trade, and commerce; energy and utility systems; waterways and modes of transportation; telecommunications and the internet: they are all managed, regulated, and communicating with one another. At their best they function reliably in the background, supporting our well-being and our peaceful coexistence. At their worst they reinforce injustice and perpetuate suffering.

There is no question that these institutions and systems must be upgraded to include the changing values of our times. Certainly, some are in more immediate need of reform than others. But before we talk about changes, we should marvel at the absolute miracle of how modern societies have organized themselves to execute and deliver such an unfathomable array of complex, interlocking functions and services that support quality of life for billions of people.

But some institutions are unjust. These must be scrutinized, evaluated, and overhauled. The work done by the Utah Task Force on Racial and Ethnic Fairness is an example of how systemic institutional change can happen. It occurs because people who interact with and value the institutions insist that change is needed. So a task force is established and people come together from within the system and join with those affected by its operation. They examine the criminal justice process in fine detail, locating points of leverage and implementing changes, redesigning the system to be less biased. This entire process relies on ongoing conversation, building relationships, and problem-solving together. It can take years, requiring multiple initiatives and sustained efforts.

Institutions are designed to endure well beyond any person or group of people who manage them at any given time. They rely on stability and reliability, so they tend to be fixed and, to some degree, unyielding. This allows them to outlast trends, personalities, and politics. But when systems are dysfunctional, change is needed. And with sustained persistence, they can evolve—if and when the people within them insist on it, and when pressure from the outside demands it.

Boundless Compassion

Enhance our awareness, evolve our skills, transform our culture, and redesign our systems and institutions—it seems like an overwhelmingly tall order. It would be if we had to do it alone, but we don't; we're in it together.

Sometimes in our Zen practice we invoke the presence of Kanzeon, also known as Guanyin, the Bodhisattva of Compassion. Her name means "She who hears the cries of the world."[9] She is often represented as having a thousand arms and hands, and in the palm of each hand is an eye with which she sees each situation with clarity, precision, and wisdom. She holds many different tools and implements so she can respond skillfully to relieve the suffering of beings everywhere. Kanzeon's capacities are unlimited, her compassion is boundless, and her care extends in all directions.

When we engage deeply in conversation, our listening becomes like Kanzeon's. When we respond to the suffering world together, we see how many arms and hands we have, and how many tools are at our disposal. When we all use our eyes to see, we see broadly, with intelligence and tremendous wisdom. Like Kanzeon, we have an unlimited capacity.

Julian is working on climate change. Rebecca is training facilitators. Michael is changing the justice system. Julia is building bridges within the interfaith council. Rob is supporting personal transformation. Lisa is doing healing work. Mark is providing leadership. Randee is teaching about power dynamics. Greg is inspiring audiences through music and art. Ken Wilber is continuing to provide maps that help us navigate new and rocky terrain. Willie is keeping it real. This is the power of a shared vision, mutual effort, and the full recognition of our interdependence.

THE PRACTICE

Commit to just one issue that matters to you. It could be racial justice, student debt, or climate change. Pick only one but commit to acting for change in all four quadrants of experience.

Enhance Awareness

Pay attention to your interior experience of the issue: your thoughts, feelings, and belief system. Engage a practice that helps you upgrade your thinking (read the latest research), relax your mind (meditation), or invite healing (somatic or psychotherapy). The emphasis here is addressing your own interior awareness.

Evolve Skills

Identify a skill that would increase your effectiveness on this issue and develop it. It could be something like better listening skills, improving your Spanish, or learning to code so that you can program compassion into technology. The point here is that each of us has the capacity to develop the skill set that will support our social action.

Engage Culture

Engage in dialogue about your issue, and learn to have truthful, compassionate, and fulfilling conversations—ones that allow people to fully participate and learn from their experience. This will require an ongoing commitment to your awareness and your conversational skill set, and you must be willing to make mistakes, learn from them, and keep going.

Transform Systems

The emphasis here is on contributing to big picture changes in systems and institutions. For this you will need patience, forbearance, and an ability to take the longest possible view on the issue. Give attention, energy, and money to an organization that helps you understand the complexity of your issue and has developed strategies for addressing the challenges over time.

Acknowledgments

We want to thank the people who have been helpful in bringing this book to print:

Jeff Salzman, Terry Patten, and Greg Thomas were extremely helpful in clarifying some of the ideas related to Integral Theory and its application to these conversations.

Randee Levine generously shared her teachings and experience regarding power relationships.

Our friends in the Freedom and Fairness workshops and online classes have given us confidence that compassionate conversations matter. We want to thank them for their sincere desire to learn, grow, and evolve our relationships.

Lisa Hartwick offered her wisdom and supported our faith in the tremendous importance of healing.

Willie Hamilton Smith provided us with excellent stories, insights, and wit.

A very special thank-you to Julia Sati, who refined our ideas and proofread the first draft with her unique devotion and rigor.

Much gratitude to our Shambhala editor, Sarah Stanton, for her interest in the content of this book.

Finally, we wish to extend our gratitude and love to Michael Zimmerman, Denise and Robert Wilson, Nado, Vovó, Alana Felt, Jenny, Swee-Im, and David for their wholehearted support.

Notes

I. Conversations Evolve

1 Ken Wilber, *The Religion of Tomorrow: A Vision for the Future of the Great Traditions—More Inclusive, More Comprehensive, More Complete* (Boulder: Shambhala, 2018), 685n3.

2 Wilber, *Religion of Tomorrow*, 206.

3 Viviane Richter, "The Big Five Mass Extinctions," *Cosmos*, https://cosmosmagazine.com/palaeontology/big-five-extinctions.

4 Robert M. Sapolsky, *Behave: The Biology of Humans at Our Best and Worst* (New York: Penguin, 2017), 22–23.

5 Daniel J. Siegel, *The Developing Mind: Toward a Neurobiology of Interpersonal Experience* (New York: Guilford Press, 2012), 28.

6 "Human Evolution Timeline Interactive," Smithsonian Museum of Natural History, http://humanorigins.si.edu/evidence/human-evolution-timeline-interactive.

7 Jean Gebser, *The Ever-Present Origin, trans. Noel Barstad and Algis Mickunas* (Athens, OH: Ohio University Press, 1997).

8 Barbara J. King, "When Did Human Speech Evolve?" NPR, September 5, 2013, www.npr.org/sections/13.7/2013/09/05/219236801/when-did-human-speech-evolve.

9 Seymour Drescher, *Abolition: A History of Slavery and Antislavery* (New York: Cambridge University Press, 2009).

10 Steven Pinker, "Is the World Getting Better or Worse? A Look at the Numbers," TED, May 21, 2018, video, 18:32, www.youtube.com/watch?v=yCm9NgobbEQ.

11 Darryl Fears, "One Million Species Face Extinction, U.N. Report Says. And Humans Will Suffer as a Result," *Washington Post,* May 6, 2019, www.washington

post.com/climate-environment/2019/05/06/one-million-species-face-extinction
-un-panel-says-humans-will-suffer-result.

12 Don E. Beck and Christopher C. Cowan, *Spiral Dynamics: Mastering Values, Leadership, and Change* (Malden, MA: Blackwell Publishing, 2011), 260–73.

13 "Summary for Policymakers of IPCC Special Report on Global Warming of 1.5°C Approved by Governments," IPCC, October 8, 2018, www.ipcc.ch/news_and_events/pr_181008_P48_spm.shtml.

14 In recent decades, conflict researchers have continued to advance theories about which competencies and skills are most conducive to the constructive management of conflict in the face of the world's increasing complexity, dynamism, and unpredictability. Peter T. Coleman, "Conflict intelligence and systemic wisdom: Meta-competencies for engaging conflict in a complex, dynamic world," *Negotiation Journal* 34, no. 1 (2018): 7–35, https://doi.org/10.1111/nejo.12211.

2. What We Have in Common

1 His Holiness the Dalai Lama, "Principal Commitments," www.dalailama.com/the
-dalai-lama/biography-and-daily-life/three-main-commitments.

2 Erika Engelhaupt, "How Human Violence Stacks Up against Other Killer Animals," *National Geographic*, September 28, 2016, https://news.national geographic.com/2016/09/human-violence-evolution-animals-nature-science.

3 Miller McPherson, Lynn Smith-Lovin, and James M. Cook, "Birds of a feather: Homophily in social networks," *Annual Review of Sociology* 27, no. 1 (2001): 415–44, https://doi.org/10.1146/annurev.soc.27.1.415.

4 A. F. Arnsten, M. A. Raskind, F. B. Taylor, and D. F. Connor, "The effects of stress exposure on prefrontal cortex: Translating basic research into successful treatments for post-traumatic stress disorder," *Neurobiology of Stress* 1 (2014): 89–99.

5 Charles Duhigg, "What Google Learned from Its Quest to Build the Perfect Team," *New York Times*, February 25, 2016, www.nytimes.com/2016/02/28 /magazine/what-google-learned-from-its-quest-to-build-the-perfect-team.html.

6 Karen Armstrong, *Buddha* (New York: Penguin, 2001), 6.

7 Armstrong, *Buddha*, 80.

8 Armstrong, *Buddha*, 83–84.

3. An Exploration of Difference

1 Ezra Klein and Robert Sapolsky, "Robert Sapolsky on the Toxic Intersection of Poverty and Stress," January 23, 2019, in *The Ezra Klein Show*, produced by Vox Media, Inc., podcast, https://podcasts.apple.com/gd/podcast/robert-sapolsky-on
-toxic-intersection-poverty-stress/id1081584611?i=1000428368813.

2 Klein and Sapolsky, "Poverty and Stress."

3 Robert W. Sussman, *The Myth of Race: The Troubling Persistence of an Unscientific Idea* (Cambridge, MA: Harvard University Press, 2017).

4 Elizabeth Dorrance Hall, "Why We Judge Others," *Psychology Today*, May 11, 2018, www.psychologytoday.com/us/blog/conscious-communication/201805/why-we-judge-others.

5 Bessel van der Kolk, MD, *The Body Keeps the Score: Brain, Mind and Body in the Healing of Trauma* (New York: Penguin, 2015), loc. 1041, Kindle.

6 Van der Kolk, *Body Keeps the Score*, loc. 1531.

7 Jena McGregor, "To Improve Diversity, Don't Make People Go to Diversity Training. Really," *Washington Post*, July 1, 2016, www.washingtonpost.com/news/on-leadership/wp/2016/07/01/to-improve-diversity-dont-make-people-go-to-diversity-training-really-2.

8 McGregor, "Diversity Training."

9 Alan Watkins, *Coherence: The Secret Science of Brilliant Leadership* (London: Kogan Page, 2015).

10 Diane Musho Hamilton, "Calming Your Brain during Conflict," *Harvard Business Review*, December 22, 2015, https://hbr.org/2015/12/calming-your-brain-during-conflict.

4. Intimacy with Identity

1 Peter Weinreich and Wendy Saunderson, *Analysing Identity Cross-cultural, Societal and Clinical Contexts* (London: Routledge, 2002), 80.

2 Natalie Morad, "Part 1: How to Be an Adult—Kegan's Theory of Adult Development," *Medium*, November 19, 2017, https://medium.com/@NataliMorad/how-to-be-an-adult-kegans-theory-of-adult-development-d63f4311b553.

3 Joel Goldberg, "It Takes a Village to Determine the Origins of an African Proverb," NPR, July 30, 2016, www.npr.org/sections/goatsandsoda/2016/07/30/487925796/it-takes-a-village-to-determine-the-origins-of-an-african-proverb.

4 Don E. Beck and Christopher C. Cowan, *Spiral Dynamics: Mastering Values, Leadership, and Change* (Malden, MA: Blackwell Publishing, 2006), 268.

5 *Kosmos* is a Greek word meaning the entire world—the physical, emotional, mental, and spiritual. Wilber, *Religion of Tomorrow*, 666n1.

6 Thomas F. Cleary and J. C. Cleary, trans., *The Blue Cliff Record* (Boston: Shambhala, 2005), 1.

7 Jack Wintz, OFM, "A Closer Look at the Peace Prayer of Saint Francis," www.franciscanmedia.org/a-closer-look-at-the-peace-prayer-of-saint-francis.

5. What Is True: The Importance of "I," "You," and "It"

1 Ken Wilber, "What Are the Four Quadrants?" *Integral Life*, October 28, 2014, https://integrallife.com/four-quadrants.

2 Diane Musho Hamilton, *Everything Is Workable: A Zen Approach to Conflict Resolution* (Boston: Shambhala, 2013), 62–66.

3   Neil deGrasse Tyson, "Science in America—Neil DeGrasse Tyson," StarTalk, April 19, 2017, video, www.youtube.com/watch?v=8MqTOEospf0&t=11s.

4   Hamilton, *Everything Is Workable*, 93–98.

5   Hamilton, *Everything Is Workable*, 85.

6   John Cook et al., "Consensus on Consensus: A Synthesis of Consensus Estimates on Human-Caused Global Warming," *Environmental Research Letters* 11, no. 4 (2016): https://doi.org/10.1088/1748-9326/11/4/048002.

7   Ken Wilber, "Excerpt A: An Integral Age at the Leading Edge," 2006, 43–45, www .kenwilber.com/Writings/PDF/ExcerptA_KOSMOS_2003.pdf.

8   Ken Wilber, *Trump and a Post-Truth World* (Boulder: Shambhala, 2017), 30.

9   Joel Stein, "How Trolls Are Ruining the Internet," *Time*, August 18, 2016, http://time.com/4457110/internet-trolls/.

10 Wilber, *Trump*, 30.

11 Kevin Roose, "The Business of Internet Outrage," *New York Times*, October 31, 2018, www.nytimes.com/2018/10/31/podcasts/the-daily/mad-world-news-face book-internet-anger.html.

6. Having a Clear Intention

1   Stephen Mitchell, *The Enlightened Mind: An Anthology of Sacred Prose* (New York: Harper Perennial, 1993), 101.

2   Sapolsky, *Behave*, 45.

3   Wilber, *Religion of Tomorrow*, 190–91.

4   Daniel Coyle, *The Talent Code: Greatness Isn't Born. It's Grown. Here's How* (New York: Bantam Books, 2009), 18.

7. Conversation Essentials

1   "Lloyd Fickett & Associates, Inc.," The Collaborative Way®, https://www.collab orativeway.com/what-is-the-collaborative-way/.

2   Lloyd Fickett and Jason Fickett, *The Collaborative Way: A Story about Engaging the Mind and Spirit of a Company* (LF & A Publishers, 1996).

3   Marshall B. Rosenberg, *Nonviolent Communication: A Language of Life* (Encinitas, CA: PuddleDancer Press, 2015).

4   Rosenberg, *Nonviolent Communication*, 13–14.

5   His Holiness the Dalai Lama, "A Human Approach to World Peace," www.dalai lama.com/messages/world-peace/a-human-approach-to-world-peace.

6   Diane Musho Hamilton, *The Zen of You and Me: A Guide to Getting Along with Just about Anyone* (Boulder: Shambhala, 2017), 39–48.

7   Greg Thomas, "360° Collaborative Leadership," www.jazzleadershipproject.com.

8   Rosenberg, *Nonviolent Communication*, 49–64.

9   Duhigg, "What Google Learned."

10 Pierre Teilhard de Chardin, *Hymn of the Universe* (New York: Harper and Row, 1961).

11 Andrew J. Clarendon, "Love's Fire: Angels in the Divine Comedy," www.angelus .online/en_US/6221/88752/love's_fire:_angels_in_the_divine_comedy.html.

8. Hidden Biases

1 Mahzarin R. Banaji and Anthony G. Greenwald, *Blindspot: Hidden Biases of Good People* (New York: Bantam Books, 2016).

2 Criminal Justice Facts, www.sentencingproject.org/criminal-justice-facts.

3 Derald Wing Sue et al., "Racial Microaggressions in Everyday Life: Implications for Clinical Practice," *American Psychologist* 62, no. 4 (2007), https://doi.org /10.1037/0003-066x.62.4.271.

4 Utah Judicial Council's Task Force on Racial and Ethnic Fairness in the Legal System, "Racial and Ethnic Fairness: Report on the State of the Criminal and Juvenile Justice System," www.utcourts.gov/specproj/retaskforce/docs/Report final.pdf.

5 Bailey Maryfield, "Implicit Racial Bias," www.jrsa.org/pubs/factsheets/jrsa-fact sheet-implicit-racial-bias.pdf.

6 National Center for State Courts, www.ncsc.org/topics/access-and-fairness /gender-and-racial-fairness/resource-guide.aspx.

7 Daniel Kahneman, *Thinking, Fast and Slow* (New York: Farrar, Straus and Giroux, 2015).

8 Seng-Ts'an, *Hsin-hsin Ming: Verses on the Faith-Mind*, trans. Richard B. Clarke (Buffalo, NY: White Pine Press, 2001).

9. A History of Injury

1 Barbara F. Walter, "Conflict Relapse and the Sustainability of Post-Conflict Peace," World Development Report 2011, http://web.worldbank.org/archive/website01306 /web/pdf/wdr background paper_walter_0.pdf.

2 Bessel van der Kolk, MD, "In Terror's Grip: Healing the Ravages of Trauma," www.traumacenter.org/products/pdf_files/terrors_grip.pdf. Additional resources on trauma can be found at David Baldwin's Trauma Information Pages, www .trauma-pages.com/.

3 Zen Peacemakers, "The Three Tenets," https://zenpeacemakers.org/the three -tenets/.

4 Jon Swaine, Oliver Laughland, and Jamiles Lartey, "Black Americans Killed by Police Twice as Likely to Be Unarmed as White People," *Guardian*, June 1, 2015, www.theguardian.com/us-news/2015/jun/01/black-americans-killed-by-police -analysis.

5 Student Peace Alliance, "Restorative Justice Training: Peace Circles," www.student peacealliance.org/uploads/2/9/4/4/29446231/peace_circles-3.pdf.

6 For more information on Kay Pranis's work and her publications, refer to the Center for Justice and Peacebuilding, https://emu.edu/cjp.

7 Frederick S. Perls, *Gestalt Therapy Verbatim* (Highland, NY: Center for Gestalt Development, 1992), 37.

8 Dzigar Kongtrul Rinpoche, "Opening the Injured Heart," *Tricycle*, Fall 2018, https://tricycle.org/magazine/buddhist-teachings-on-tsewa.

10. Strong Emotions in Conversation

1 Daniel Goleman, *Emotional Intelligence: Why It Can Matter More than IQ, 10th Anniversary Edition* (New York: Bantam Books, 2005).

2 Peg Streep, "Six Things You Need to Know about Empathy," *Psychology Today*, January 2017, www.psychologytoday.com/us/blog/tech-support/201701/6-things -you-need-know-about-empathy.

3 Goleman, *Emotional Intelligence*, 6–7.

4 Hamilton, "Calming."

5 Sapolsky, *Behave*, 125–34; Sarah Klein, "The 3 Major Stress Hormones, Explained," Huffington Post, April 19, 2013, www.huffpost.com/entry/adrenaline-cortisol -stress-hormones_n_3112800.

6 Robert Augustus Masters, *Emotional Intimacy: A Comprehensive Guide for Connecting with the Power of Your Emotions* (Louisville, CO: Sounds True, 2013), 155.

7 Robin J. DiAngelo, *White Fragility: Why It's So Hard for White People to Talk about Racism* (Boston: Beacon Press, 2018).

8 DiAngelo, *White Fragility*, 103.

9 Karla McLaren, "Your Emotional Vocabulary List," www.karlamclaren.com/emo tional-vocabulary-page/; also see Karla McLaren, *Language of Emotions: What Your Feelings Are Trying to Tell You* (Louisville, CO: Sounds True, 2010).

10 Matthew D. Lieberman et al., "Putting Feelings into Words," *Psychological Science* 18, no. 5 (2007): https://doi.org/10.1111/j.1467-9280.2007.01916.x; Matthew D. Lieberman et al., "Subjective responses to emotional stimuli during labeling, reappraisal, and distraction," *Emotion* 11, no. 3 (2011): https://doi.org/10.1037/a0023503.

11 Rick Hanson and Richard Mendius, *Buddha's Brain: The Practical Neuroscience of Happiness, Love, and Wisdom* (Oakland, CA: New Harbinger Publications, 2009).

12 Michael Bergeisen, "The Neuroscience of Happiness," *Greater Good Magazine* (blog), Greater Good Science Center at UC Berkeley, September 22, 2010, https://greatergood.berkeley.edu/article/item/the_neuroscience_of_happiness.

11. Clarifying Power

1 Wilber, *Religion of Tomorrow*, 129.

2 Amy and Arnold Mindell, "Process-Oriented Psychology," www.aamindell.net /process-work.

3 Mary Parker Follett, *Dynamic Administration: The Collected Papers of Mary Parker Follett* (1940; repr., Mansfield Centre, CT: Martino Publishing, 2013).

4 Sapolsky, *Behave*, 425–77.

12. Talking about Social Privilege

1 W. E. B. Du Bois and David Levering Lewis (introduction), *Black Reconstruction in America: Toward a History of the Part Which Black Folk Played in the Attempt to Reconstruct Democracy in America, 1860–1880* (New York: The Free Press, 1935, 1992), 700–701. A copy of this book is available online at https://libcom.org/files/black_reconstruction_an_essay_toward_a_history_of_.pdf.

2 Ralph Keyes, *The Quote Verifier: Who Said What, Where, and When* (New York: St. Martin's Press, 2006), 17.

3 Food Empowerment Project, "Child Labor and Slavery in the Chocolate Industry," www.foodispower.org/slavery-chocolate/.

4 Michelle Chen, "The Democratic Republic of Congo's Other Crisis," *Nation*, January 27, 2019, www.thenation.com/article/congo-china-mining-electronics/.

5 Kwame Anthony Appiah, *The Ethics of Identity* (Princeton, NJ: Princeton University Press, 2010).

6 Martin Luther King Jr., "Letter from a Birmingham Jail," http://okra.stanford.edu/transcription/document_images/undecided/630416-019.pdf.

7 Peggy McIntosh, "White Privilege and Male Privilege: A Personal Account of Coming to See Correspondences through Work in Women's Studies," *Working Paper* no. 189 (Center for Research on Women, 1988).

8 Armstrong, *Buddha*, 6.

9 Thanissaro Bhikkhu, trans., "Chiggala Sutta, The Hole," www.buddhasutra.com/files/chiggala_sutta.htm.

10 Alex Grey, "The Vast Expanse," https://www.alexgrey.com/media/writing/art-psalms/the-vast-expanse.

13. Politically Correct

1 Walpola Sri Rahula, "The Noble Eightfold Path: Meaning and Practice," *Tricycle*, https://tricycle.org/magazine/noble-eightfold-path/.

2 Wilber, *Trump*, 26.

3 Chris Gethard, "Political Correctness in Comedy: Is It Making Us Too Afraid to Be Funny?" Big Think, July 6, 2016, video, www.youtube.com/watch?v=FjRBHS9nOlw.

4 George Carlin, *When Will Jesus Bring the Pork Chops?* (New York: Hyperion, 2005), 69.

5 Joe Rogan (@joerogan), "Recreational outrage is obviously running out of targets. Hoop earrings criticized as cultural appropriation," Twitter, October 18, 2017, https://twitter.com/joerogan/status/920734179557507073.

6 Zephyr Teachout, "I'm Not Convinced Franken Should Quit," *New York Times*, December 11, 2017, www.nytimes.com/2017/12/11/opinion/franken-resignation -harassment-democrats.html.

7 Laura Kipnis, "Kick against the Pricks," *New York Review of Books*, December 21, 2017, www.nybooks.com/articles/2017/12/21/kick-against-the-pricks/. Valeriya Safronova, "Catherine Deneuve and Others Denounce the #MeToo Movement," *New York Times*, January 9, 2018, www.nytimes.com/2018/01/09/movies/catherine -deneuve-and-others-denounce-the-metoo-movement.html.

8 "But every approach, I honestly believe, is essentially true but partial, true but partial, true but partial. And on my own tombstone, I dearly hope that some-day they will write: He was true but partial." Ken Wilber, *Collected Works of Ken Wilber: Vol. 8* (Boston: Shambhala, 2000), 49.

9 Douglas Stone, Sheila Heen, and Bruce Patton, *Difficult Conversations: How to Discuss What Matters Most* (New York: Penguin, 2010), 44–57.

14. Growing through Conflict

1 Robert Kegan, *In Over Our Heads: The Mental Demands of Modern Life* (Cambridge, MA: Harvard University Press, 1994), 319.

2 Ken Wilber, *A Brief History of Everything* (Boston: Shambhala, 2000), 237–38.

3 Victor Hugo, *The History of a Crime (Histoire d'un crime): The Testimony of an Eyewitness*, trans. T. H. Joyce and Arthur Locker (New York: Mondial, 2005).

4 Connie Peck and Eleanor Wertheim, eds., "Understanding the Sources of Conflict. Strengthening the Practice of Peacemaking and Preventive Diplomacy in the United Nations: The UNITAR Approach," 13–22, https://unitar.org/pmcp/sites /unitar.org.pmcp/files/sppd.pdf.

5 Josh Gabbatis, "Brexit Is Strongly Linked to Xenophobia, According to Scientists," *Independent*, November 28, 2017, www.independent.co.uk/news/science/brexit -prejudice-scientists-link-foreigners-immigrants-racism-xenophobia-leave -eu-a8078586.html. Damien Gayle, "UK Has Seen 'Brexit-Related' Growth in Racism, Says UN Representative," *Guardian*, May 11, 2018, www.theguardian.com /politics/2018/may/11/uk-has-seen-brexit-related-growth-in-racism-says-un -representative.

6 Paulo Freire, *Pedagogy of the Oppressed* (New York: Bloomsbury, 2018).

7 His Holiness the Dalai Lama, *How to Be Compassionate: A Handbook for Creating Inner Peace and a Happier World*, ed. and trans. Jeffrey Hopkins (New York: Atria Books, 2011), 18.

8 Ben Schreckinger, "Kids of Republicans Pull Parents to the Left on Gay Marriage," *Politico*, April 27, 2015, www.politico.com/story/2015/04/republicans-gay-marriage -117400.

9 Liam Stack, "A Brief History of Deadly Attacks on Abortion Providers," *New York Times*, November 29, 2015, www.nytimes.com/interactive/2015/11/29/us/30 abortion-clinic-violence.html.

10 Ann Fowler et al., "Talking with the Enemy," www.feminist.com/resources/art speech/genwom/talkingwith.html.

11 Jonah Engel Bromwich, "Everyone Is Canceled," *New York Times*, June 28, 2018, www.nytimes.com/2018/06/28/style/is-it-canceled.html.

12 Wilber, *Brief History*, 110–22.

13 Steven Pinker, *The Better Angels of Our Nature: Why Violence Has Declined* (New York: Penguin Books, 2012).

15. Shadow in Conversation

1 "The Jungian Model of the Psyche," *Journal Psyche*, http://journalpsyche.org /jungian-model-psyche/.

2 "The History of Keffiyeh: A Traditional Scarf from Palestine," https://hand madepalestine.com/blogs/news/history-of-keffiyeh-the-traditional-palestinian -headdress.

3 Elias Jahshan, "So, You Want to Wear a Keffiyeh?" *Alaraby*, February 13, 2018, www.alaraby.co.uk/english/comment/2018/2/13/so-you-want-to-wear-a-keffiyeh.

4 Stephen B. Karpman, *A Game Free Life: The Definitive Book on the Drama Triangle and the Compassion Triangle by the Originator and Author* (San Francisco, CA: Drama Triangle Productions, 2014).

5 Diane Musho Hamilton, "3-2-1 Shadow Process," *Integral Life*, https://integrallife .com/tag/3-2-1-process/.

16. Miraculously Resilient

1 Alqumit Alhamad, "Artist and LGTBQ Activist," TEDxFolketspark, August 29, 2017, video, www.youtube.com/watch?v=4wY81_RzLpo. Alqumit Alhamad, "Sexuality, Violence, and Beauty in Art: Interview with Alqumit Alhamad," *Queer Asia* (blog), July 12, 2018, https://queerasia.com/qa18art-blog-alhamad/.

2 "The Road to Resilience," American Psychological Association, www.apa.org /helpcenter/road-resilience.

3 Ann S. Masten, Wendy K. Silverman, and Joy D. Osofsky, "Children in War and Disaster," in *Handbook of Child Psychology and Developmental Science*, ed. Richard M. Lerner, 7th ed., vol. 3 (Hoboken, NJ: Wiley, 2015), 704–37. William C. Nichols, "Roads to Understanding Family Resilience: 1920s to the Twenty-First Century," in *Handbook of Family Resilience*, ed. Dorothy Becvar (New York: Springer, 2013), 3–16.

4 Van der Kolk, *Body Keeps the Score*.

5 Stephen W. Porges, *The Pocket Guide to the Polyvagal Theory: The Transformative Power of Feeling Safe* (New York: W. W. Norton, 2017).

6 Peter A. Levine, *Waking the Tiger: Healing Trauma, the Innate Capacity to Transform Overwhelming Experiences* (Berkeley, CA: North Atlantic Books, 1997).

7 Martin E. P. Seligman, *The Optimistic Child: A Proven Program to Safeguard*

Children against Depression and Build Lifelong Resilience (New York: Houghton Mifflin, 2007).

8 Bessel van der Kolk, "The Body Keeps the Score: Memory and the Evolving Psychobiology of Posttraumatic Stress," *Harvard Review of Psychiatry* 1, no. 5 (1994), https://doi.org/10.3109/10673229409017088.

9 Ilyssa Wellikoff, "Victim-Offender Mediation and Violent Crimes: On the Way to Justice," *Cardozo Journal of Conflict Resolution*, vol. 5.1 (Fall 2003): https://car dozojcr.com/issues/volume-5-1/note-1/.

10 Van der Kolk, "Body Keeps the Score"; Levine, *Waking the Tiger*.

11 Pieter Hugo, "Portraits of Reconciliation," *New York Times*, April 4, 2014, www .nytimes.com/interactive/2014/04/06/magazine/06-pieter-hugo-rwanda-portraits .html.

12 Hugo, "Portraits of Reconciliation."

13 Pema Chödrön, *Start Where You Are: A Guide to Compassionate Living* (Boston: Shambhala, 1994, 2018), 38–43; Hamilton, *Everything Is Workable*, 93–98.

17. To Atone and Forgive

1 Theo Dawson, "Measuring Complexity: A Short History," https://medium.com /@theo_dawson/our-place-in-the-piagetian-timeline-30cb39931f62.

2 Nelson Mandela, *Long Walk to Freedom: The Autobiography of Nelson Mandela* (New York: Little, Brown, 1994), 622.

3 "Tutu and His Role in the Truth and Reconciliation Commission," South African History Online, www.sahistory.org.za/article/tutu-and-his-role-truth-reconcilia tion-commission.

4 Desmond Tutu, "Forgiveness: What Do You Do to Forgive Someone?" Desmond Tutu Peace Foundation, November 11, 2012, video, 4:25, www.youtube.com/watch ?v=uo2LGGqtjqM.

5 Shohaku Okumura, *Living by Vow: A Practical Introduction to Eight Essential Zen Chants and Texts* (Boston: Wisdom Publications, 2012), 54.

6 Giovanni Novembre, Marco Zanon, and Giorgia Silani, "Empathy for Social Exclusion Involves the Sensory-Discriminative Component of Pain: A Within-Subject FMRI Study," *Social Cognitive and Affective Neuroscience* 10, no. 2 (2014): 153–64.

7 Desmond Tutu, "Forgiveness."

8 PCDN, "Martin Luther King Jr. on Forgiveness," https://pcdnetwork.org/blogs /martin-luther-king-jr-on-forgiveness/.

9 Linda Graham, "How to Overcome Barriers to Forgiveness," *Greater Good Magazine*, May 13, 2014, https://greatergood.berkeley.edu/article/item/overcome _barriers_forgiveness.

10 Thomas W. Baskin and Robert D. Enright, "Intervention Studies on Forgiveness: A Meta-Analysis," *Journal of Counseling and Development* 82, no. 1 (2004): 79–90.

11 Martin Luther King Jr., "Loving Your Enemies," https://kinginstitute.stanford

.edu/king-papers/documents/loving-your-enemies-sermon-delivered-dexter
-avenue-baptist-church.

12 Martin Luther King Jr., *A Gift of Love: Sermons from Strength to Love and Other Preachings* (Boston: Beacon, 1981, 2012), 35.

18. Becoming Wholehearted

1 Diane Musho Hamilton, "Everything Is Workable—A Zen Approach to Conflict Resolution," Talks at Google, June 13, 2014, video, 47:56, https://www.youtube.com /watch?v=UDekZGJ5Y-c.

2 Thich Nhat Hanh, *True Love: A Practice for Awakening the Heart* (Boston: Shambhala, 2004), 67–69.

3 Thich Nhat Hanh, *True Love,* 70.

4 Anodea Judith, *Eastern Body, Western Mind: Psychology and the Chakra System as a Path to the Self* (Berkeley, CA: Celestial Arts, 2004), 221–83.

5 Paul R. Goldin, "Xunzi," *Stanford Encyclopedia of Philosophy*, https://plato .stanford.edu/entries/xunzi/#HearMindXin.

6 bell hooks, "Toward a Worldwide Culture of Love," *Lion's Roar*, October 12, 2018, www.lionsroar.com/toward-a-worldwide-culture-of-love/.

7 Doc Childre, Howard Martin, Deborah Rozman, and Rollin McCraty, *Heart Intelligence: Connecting with the Intuitive Guidance of the Heart* (Waterfront Digital Press, 2017), 21.

8 Daniel Goleman, *Destructive Emotions: A Scientific Dialogue with the Dalai Lama* (New York: Bantam Books, 2003), 161.

9 Natalie Frank, "Who Said the Phrase 'Holding a Grudge Is like Drinking Poison and Waiting for the Other Person to Die'?," Quora, July 5, 2016, https://www .quora.com/Who-said-the-phrase-Holding-a-grudge-is-like-drinking-poison -and-waiting-for-the-other-person-to-die.

10 Tania Singer and Olga M. Klimecki, "Empathy and Compassion," *Current Biology* 24, no. 18 (2014): R875–78, https://doi.org/10.1016/j.cub.2014.06.054.

11 C. Daniel Bateson, "These Things Called Empathy: Eight Related but Distinct Phenomena," in *Social Neuroscience of Empathy*, ed. Jean Decety and William Ickes (Cambridge, MA: MIT Press, 2011), 3–15.

12 Singer et al., "Empathy."

13 The Chopra Center, "What's the Difference Between Empathy, Sympathy, and Compassion?" https://chopra.com/articles/whats-the-difference-between -empathy-sympathy-and-compassion.

14 Hyeonjin Jeon and Seung-Hwan Lee, "From neurons to social beings: Short review of the mirror neuron system research and its socio-psychological and psychiatric implications," *Clinical Psychopharmacology and Neuroscience* 16, no. 1 (2018): 18–31, https://doi.org/10.9758/cpn.2018.16.1.18.

15 Goleman, *Destructive Emotions.*

16 The Chopra Center, "What's the Difference?"

17 Thich Nhat Hanh, *Transformation and Healing: Sutra on the Four Establishments of Mindfulness* (Berkeley, CA: Parallax Press, 2006), 71.

18 Martin Luther King Jr., "I've Been to the Mountaintop," April 3, 1968, Memphis, TN, https://kinginstitute.stanford.edu/encyclopedia/ive-been-mountaintop.

19 Martin Luther King Jr., "I Have a Dream," August 28, 1963, Washington, DC, https://kinginstitute.stanford.edu/king-papers/documents/i-have-dream-address -delivered-march-washington-jobs-and-freedom.

19. Freedom Here and Now

1 Diane Musho Hamilton, "A Zen Approach to Conflict Resolution."

2 Karl Marx, "A Contribution to the Critique of Hegel's Philosophy of Right," Dec. 1843–Jan. 1844, www.marxists.org/archive/marx/works/1843/critique-hpr/intro.htm.

3 Emma Varvaloucas, "Okay as It Is, Okay as You Are," *Tricycle*, Fall 2013, https://tri cycle.org/magazine/okay-it-okay-you-are/.

4 Mary B. Anderson, *Do No Harm: How Aid Can Support Peace—or War* (Boulder: Lynne Rienner, 1999); *Séverine Autesserre, Peaceland: Conflict Resolution and the Everyday Politics of International Intervention* (New York: Cambridge University Press, 2014).

5 Arbinger Institute, *The Anatomy of Peace: Resolving the Heart of Conflict* (Oakland, CA: Berrett-Koehler, 2015).

6 Kelsey Moss, private communication with Gabe Wilson and Kim Loh.

7 Norman Fischer, "Beyond Language," *Tricycle*, Summer 2011, https://tricycle.org /magazine/beyond-language/.

8 His Holiness the Dalai Lama, *How to Practice: The Way to a Meaningful Life*, ed. Jeffrey Hopkins (New York: Atria Books, 2003), 39.

20. In It Together

1 Beck and Cowan, *Spiral Dynamics*, 12.

2 Daniel J. Siegel, *Aware: The Science and Practice of Presence* (New York: TarcherPerigee, 2018), 4–5.

3 Wayne W. Dyer, "Success Secrets," www.drwaynedyer.com/blog/success-secrets/.

4 Marcel M. Robles, "Executive perceptions of the top 10 soft skills needed in to-day's workplace," *Business Communication Quarterly 75*, no. 4 (2012): https://doi .org/10.1177/1080569912460400.

5 Zen Master Dogen, *Treasury of the True Dharma Eye: Zen Master Dōgen's Shobo Genzo*, ed. Kazuaki Tanahashi (Boston: Shambhala, 2013), 650.

6 Hayden Carpenter, "What 'The Dawn Wall' Left Out," *Outside*, September 18, 2018, www.outsideonline.com/2344706/dawn-wall-documentary-tommy -caldwell-review.

7 Chögyam Trungpa Rinpoche, "The Bodhisattva," *Lion's Roar*, January 1, 2017, www.lionsroar.com/the-bodhisattva/.

8 John Lewis, "We Are the Beloved Community," https://onbeing.org/programs /beloved-community-john-lewis-2/.

9 "Bodhisattva Avalokitesvara: Guanyin," Dunhuang Foundation, October 26, 2017, http://dunhuangfoundation.us/blog/2017/10/18/bodhisattva-avalokitesvara -guanyin.

Selected Bibliography

Armstrong, Karen. *Buddha*. New York: Penguin, 2001.

Banaji, Mahzarin R., and Anthony G. Greenwald. *Blindspot: Hidden Biases of Good People*. New York: Bantam Books, 2016.

Beck, Don Edward, and Christopher C. Cowan. *Spiral Dynamics: Mastering Values, Leadership, and Change: Exploring the New Science of Memetics*. Malden, MA: Blackwell Publishing, 1996, 2006.

Childre, Doc, Howard Martin, Deborah Rozman, and Rollin McCraty. *Heart Intelligence: Connecting with the Intuitive Guidance of the Heart*. Buffalo, NY: Waterfront Press, 2017.

Chödrön, Pema. *Start Where You Are: A Guide to Compassionate Living*. Boston: Shambhala, 1994, 2018.

Dalai Lama, His Holiness the. *How to Be Compassionate: A Handbook for Creating Inner Peace and a Happier World*. Edited by Jeffrey Hopkins. New York: Atria Books, 2011.

———. *How to Practice: The Way to a Meaningful Life*. Edited by Jeffrey Hopkins. New York: Atria Books, 2003.

De Waal, Frans. *Our Inner Ape: A Leading Primatologist Explains Why We Are Who We Are*. New York: Riverhead Books, 2006.

Diamond, Julie. *Power: A User's Guide*. Santa Fe, NM: Belly Song Press, 2016.

DiAngelo, Robin J. *White Fragility: Why It's So Hard for White People to Talk about Racism*. Boston: Beacon Press, 2018.

Dogen, and Kazuaki Tanahashi. *Treasury of the True Dharma Eye: Zen Master Dōgen's Shobo Genzo*. Boston: Shambhala, 2013.

Du Bois, W. E. B., and David Levering Lewis (introduction). *Black Reconstruction in America: Toward a History of the Part Which Black Folk Played in the Attempt to Reconstruct Democracy in America, 1860-1880*. New York: The Free Press, 1935, 1992.

Fickett, Lloyd, and Jason Fickett. *The Collaborative Way: A Story about Engaging the Mind and Spirit of a Company*. LF & A Pub., 1996.

Freire, Paulo. *Pedagogy of the Oppressed, 50th Anniversary Edition.* Translated by Myra Bergman Ramos. New York: Bloomsbury, 2018.

Gebser, Jean, Noel Barstad, and Algis Mickunas. *The Ever-Present Origin.* Athens, OH: Ohio University Press, 1997.

Goleman, Daniel. *Destructive Emotions: A Scientific Dialogue with the Dalai Lama.* New York: Bloomsbury, 2013.

———. *Emotional Intelligence, 10th Anniversary Edition.* New York: Bantam Books, 2005.

———. *Working with Emotional Intelligence.* New York: Bantam Books, 1998.

Hamilton, Diane Musho. *Everything Is Workable: A Zen Approach to Conflict Resolution.* Boston: Shambhala, 2013.

———. *The Zen of You & Me: A Guide to Getting Along with Just About Anyone.* Boulder: Shambhala, 2017.

Hanson, Rick, and Richard Mendius. *Buddha's Brain: The Practical Neuroscience of Happiness, Love & Wisdom.* Oakland, CA: New Harbinger Publications, 2009.

Kahneman, Daniel. *Thinking, Fast and Slow.* New York: Farrar, Straus and Giroux, 2015.

Kegan, Robert. *In Over Our Heads: The Mental Demands of Modern Life.* Cambridge, MA: Harvard University Press, 1997.

Kornfield, Jack. *The Wise Heart: A Guide to the Universal Teachings of Buddhist Psychology.* New York: Bantam Books, 2009.

Levine, Peter A. *Waking the Tiger: Healing Trauma: The Innate Capacity to Transform Overwhelming Experiences.* Berkeley, CA: North Atlantic Books, 1997.

Masters, Robert Augustus. *Emotional Intimacy: A Comprehensive Guide for Connecting with the Power of Your Emotions.* Louisville, CO: Sounds True, 2013.

McLaren, Karla. *Language of Emotions.* Louisville, CO: Sounds True, 2010.

Mitchell, Stephen. *The Enlightened Mind: An Anthology of Sacred Prose.* New York: Harper Perennial, 1993.

Mandela, Nelson. *Long Walk to Freedom: The Autobiography of Nelson Mandela.* New York: Little, Brown, 1994.

Nhat Hanh, Thích, and Sherab Chödzin Kohn. *True Love: A Practice for Awakening the Heart.* Boston: Shambhala, 2011.

Okumura, Shohaku. *Living by Vow: A Practical Introduction to Eight Essential Zen Chants and Texts.* Boston: Wisdom Publications, 2012.

Pinker, Steven. *The Better Angels of Our Nature: Why Violence Has Declined.* New York: Penguin Books, 2012.

Porges, Stephen W. *The Pocket Guide to the Polyvagal Theory: The Transformative Power of Feeling Safe.* New York: W. W Norton, 2017.

Rogers, Carl R. *Active Listening.* Eastford, CT: Martino Fine Books, 2015. Reprint.

Rosenberg, Marshall B. *Nonviolent Communication: A Language of Life.* Encinitas, CA: PuddleDancer Press, 2015.

Sapolsky, Robert M. *Behave: The Biology of Humans at Our Best and Worst.* New York: Penguin, 2017.

Siegel, Daniel J. *Aware: The Science and Practice of Presence—the Groundbreaking Meditation Practice.* New York: TarcherPerigee, 2018.

———. *The Developing Mind: Toward a Neurobiology of Interpersonal Experience*. New York: Guilford Press, 2012.

Stone, Douglas, Sheila Heen, and Bruce Patton. *Difficult Conversations: How to Discuss What Matters Most*. 10th Anniversary Edition. New York: Penguin Books, 2010.

Sussman, Robert W. *The Myth of Race: The Troubling Persistence of an Unscientific Idea*. Cambridge, MA: Harvard University Press, 2017.

Van Der Kolk, Bessel A. *The Body Keeps the Score: Brain, Mind and Body in the Healing of Trauma*. New York: Penguin Books, 2015.

Watkins, Alan. *Coherence: The Secret Science of Brilliant Leadership*. London: Kogan Page, 2015.

Wilber, Ken. *A Brief History of Everything*. 2nd ed. Boston: Shambhala, 2000.

———. *The Religion of Tomorrow: A Vision for the Future of the Great Traditions—More Inclusive, More Comprehensive, More Complete*. Boulder: Shambhala, 2018.

———. *Trump and a Post-Truth World*. Boulder: Shambhala, 2017.

Index

About the Authors

Diane Musho Hamilton is an award-winning professional mediator, author, and Zen teacher in the White Plum lineage. She is the cofounder of Two Arrows Zen, a practice in Utah. She is the author of *Everything Is Workable* and *The Zen of You and Me*.

Gabriel Menegale Wilson is a leadership coach, organizational change consultant with DELTA Developmental, and Integral Facilitator researching and practicing peace. His present work focuses on educational initiatives that free human potential to address the challenges of our century.

Kimberly Myosai Loh is an author, coach, and peace specialist working to foster conflict transformation and ethical leadership. Her work includes international peace research at the United Nations, postgraduate conflict resolution at Columbia University, and individual and group coaching to expand our personal and collective potential.